MEATLESS MEALS FOR WORKING PEOPLE

Quick and Easy Vegetarian Recipes

By Debra Wasserman
& Charles Stahler

Baltimore, Maryland
Fifth Edition, 2009

Acknowledgements

Special thanks to Reed Mangels, PhD, RD, for doing the nutritional analysis for all the recipes and contributing her expertise to this book including the weekly low-cost menus. Thank you also to the following individuals who provided information: Ruth Blackburn, MS, RD, Sarah Blum, Davida Breier, Heather Gorn, Marie Henein, Suzanne Havala Hobbs, DrPH, RD, Barbara Lovitts, PhD., Jeannie McStay, Stephanie Reph, Brad Scott, Annabelle Simpson, Mama Golub-Smith, Ellen Tattenbaum, Linda Tyler, Mike Vogel, and Jeanne Yacoubou, MS. And finally, thank you to John Peters for doing the wonderful illustrations and David Herring for proofreading updated parts of this edition.

Please note: The contents of *Meatless Meals for Working People* are not intended to provide medical advice. Medical advice should be obtained from a qualified health professional.

Library of Congress Cataloging-in-Publication Data

Wasserman, Debra.
   Meatless meals for working people : quick and easy vegetarian recipes / by Debra Wasserman & Charles Stahler. -- 5th ed.
      p. cm.
   Includes index.
   Summary: "Includes quick vegetarian recipes, information on vegetarian and vegan items found at fast food and quick service chains, large restaurant chains most suitable for vegetarians, vegetarian meal plan, suggested items for vegetarian meals, vegetarian spice chart, party ideas, and vegetarianism on the job" "[summary]"--Provided by publisher.
   ISBN 978-0-931411-32-8
   1. Vegetarian cookery. 2. Quick and easy cookery. I. Stahler, Charles. II. Title.
   TX837.W32 2009
   641.5'636--dc22

                                                                    2009014299

Printed in the United States of America
10 9 8 7 6 5 4 3 2 1

Table of Contents

Salads and Dressings

Soups

Lunch Ideas

Side Dishes

Side Dishes (continued)

Main Dishes

Soy Dishes

Chinese Cuisine

Vegetarianism in a Nutshell

Vegetarianism is the abstinence from meat, fish, and fowl. Among the many reasons for being a vegetarian are compassion for animals, aesthetic considerations, and ecological, economic, spiritual, and health reasons. The American Dietetic Association has affirmed that a vegetarian diet can meet all known nutrient needs. Like every diet, the key to a healthy vegetarian diet is simple. Eat a variety of foods, eat a lot of greens, and have high-fat, high-salt, empty-calorie foods as only a small part of your diet. For the growing number of vegetarians who are following a vegan life-style and abstain from all animal products, including milk, cheese, eggs, and honey, this also can be done easily, but you may want to talk to others who have been practicing this diet.

Fresh is Best, But...

Using frozen, canned, and prepackaged foods greatly decreases food preparation time whether you are on a vegetarian diet or a non-vegetarian diet. Beware, however, that many prepackaged foods are high in sodium and may have animal shortening in them.

FROZEN FOODS

Frozen foods can be stored easily, and quickly popped into the oven while you're changing your clothes after work. Frozen vegetables such as green beans, corn, and spinach can be cooked in a short time and eaten alone or combined with other ingredients. Be careful not to overcook the vegetables or use too much water when cooking them. Several frozen pasta and vegetable mixes can be found in supermarkets, including vegetarian entrées manufactured by natural foods companies, which can be served for lunch or dinner.

CANNED AND PREPACKAGED VEGETARIAN FOODS

Though often more expensive than preparing from scratch, there are numerous canned and prepackaged foods you can find in most supermarkets. These items can quickly be used to prepare a meal or simply have a snack.

DAIRY CASE

Your dairy case is packed full of vegetarian ingredients and fast meal possibilities. Corn and wheat tortillas can easily be heated up and stuffed with leftover bean, grain, and/or vegetable mixtures.

Suggested Vegetarian Meals

Listed below are quick dishes and food items that you probably know how to cook already and can be made from common foods found in supermarkets. For a main meal, you may have one large central dish, a sandwich with or without soup, or several side dishes. Remember, the key to any healthy diet is variety.

BREAKFAST ITEMS:
These can easily be served as part of a main meal. You can substitute 1 small mashed ripe banana for each egg when making batter for French toast or using pancake and waffle mixes.

<u>Frozen Breakfast Foods</u>
Amy's Organic Toaster Pops
Bagels
Biscuits
Meatless Breakfast Patties and Links
Van's Waffles (flax, soy, etc.)

<u>Other Breakfast Foods</u>
Applesauce
Breads (English muffins, cornbread, rye, etc.)
Dry Cereal (Grape-Nuts, Muesli, Puffed Kashi, etc.)
Hot Cereal (Cream of Rice and Cream of Wheat, Farina, grits,
    oatmeal, Wheatena, etc.)
Fresh Fruit
Fruit Butters (apple butter, etc.)
Granola
Health Valley Cereal Bars
Jams (fruit sweetened variety is best)
Soy Yogurt
Wheat Germ

SANDWICHES:
Nut Butter (peanut, cashew, almond, etc.) and Jam
Bagels and Hummus (chickpea spread)
Nut Butter and Sliced Fruit (banana, apple, pear)
Sloppy Joe Sauce and Vegetables
Baked Beans and Lettuce on Toast
Tofu Salad (mashed tofu, minced celery, grated
    carrot, sweet relish, soy mayonnaise)
Chickpea Salad (mashed chickpeas, grated carrot,
    minced celery, dill weed, mayonnaise)

<u>Breads</u>
Bagels
English Muffins
French Bread
Hard Rolls
Italian Bread
Kaiser Rolls
Pita Bread
Pumpernickle Bread
Raisin Bread
Rye Bread
Tortillas
Whole Wheat Bread

MAIN MEALS (lunch or dinner):
<u>Frozen Main Dishes</u>
The following list is by no means complete, rather just a start.

Amy's Kitchen
    Asian Noodle Stir-Fry
    Organic Beans and Rice Burrito
    Organic Black Bean Vegetable Burrito
    Organic Breakfast Burrito
    Roasted Vegetable Pizza

Boca Foods Company
   Vegan Boca Burger

Gardenburger Inc.
   BBQ Riblets
   Breaded Chik'n
   Chik'n Grill
   Herb Crusted Cutlet
   Veggie Breakfast Sausage

Gardenburger Inc. Gardenburgers
   Black Bean Chipotle
   California Burger
   Flame Grilled
   GardenVegan
   Veggie Medley

Health is Wealth
   Buffalo Wings
   Chicken-Free Nuggets
   Chicken-Free Patties

Morningstar Farms
   Ground Meatless Crumbles
   Vegan Burger
   Veggie Chik'n Strips
   Veggie Steak Strips

Nate's
   Classic Flavor Meatless Meatballs
   Savory Mushroom Meatless Meatballs
   Zesty Italian Meatless Meatballs

ETHNIC FOODS FOR MAIN MEALS (LUNCH OR DINNER):

Asian
Canned Vegetables (water chestnuts, baby corn, etc.)
Coconut Milk
Mustards
Rice Noodles
Sauces and Marinades (be sure to watch out for non-vegetarian fats and broths)

Jewish
Borscht
Falafel Mix
Hummus
Kasha
Mandlen for Soup (soup nuts)
Matzo
Matzo Meal
Potato Pancakes
Soup Mixes
Tahini (sesame butter)
Tam Tam Crackers
Tea Biscuits

Mexican
Burrito and Taco Kits
Fajita Marinade
Green Chiles
Guava and Mango Paste
Salsa
Taco Sauces and Seasoning Mixes
Tortillas and Taco Shells
Vegetarian Refried Beans (without lard)

Middle Eastern
Falafel Mix
Hummus (canned)
Hummus Mix
Tahini Sauce

PASTA:

Most pasta sold in packages in supermarkets doesn't contain eggs, unless it is called "egg pasta." Please note that fresh pasta often contains eggs. Look for eggless brands including Barilla, De-Boles, Mueller's, and San Giorgio.

PASTA SAUCES:

Amy's Premium Organic Pasta Sauce
- Family Marinara
- Low Sodium Marinara
- Roasted Garlic
- Tomato Basil

Classico
- Fire-Roasted Tomato and Garlic
- Mushrooms and Ripe Olives
- Organic Spinach and Garlic
- Organic Tomato, Herbs, & Spices
- Roasted Garlic
- Spicy Red Pepper
- Sun-dried Tomato
- Tomato and Basil

Muir Glen
- Chunky Tomato and Herb
- Fire Roasted Tomato
- Garden Vegetable
- Garlic Roasted Garlic
- Italian Herb
- Portabello Mushroom
- Tomato Basil

Newman's Own
    Marinara with Mushrooms
    Organic Marinara
    Organic Tomato and Basil
    Organic Traditional Herb Sauce

Walnut Acres Certified Organic
    Garlic Garlic
    Marinara and Zinfandel
    Sweet Pepper & Onion
    Tomato and Basil

VEGETARIAN DRY MIXES TO MAKE MAIN MEALS:

Fantastic Foods
    Black Beans
    Falafel
    Hummus
    Nature's Burger
    Refried Beans
    Sloppy Joe Mix
    Tabouli
    Taco Filling
    Tofu Buger
    Vegetarian Chili

DAIRY CASE ITEMS:

Flour and Corn Tortillas
Fruit Salad in Jars
Guacamole
Juice
Rice Milk
Salsa
Soy Creamer
Soy Milk
Soy Yogurt

ITEMS FOUND IN PRODUCE SECTION BESIDES PRODUCE:
Chopped Garlic, Jalapeño Peppers, etc.
Meat Alternatives (Burgers, Deli Slices, Hot Dogs, Meatless
　　Ground, Veggie Bacon, Veggie Sausage, etc.)
Polenta
Salad Dressings
Soy Cheese
Sun-Dried Tomatoes
Tempeh
Tofu

ITEMS FOUND IN THE DELI COUNTER SECTION:
Dilled Cucumbers
Hummus
Olives
Tabouli
Vegetable Salads

SIDE DISHES:
Amy's Organic Chili
Bush's Vegetarian Baked Beans
Campbell's Vegetarian Beans in Tomato Sauce
Hanover Vegetarian Baked Beans
Heinz Vegetarian Beans in Tomato Sauce
Old El Paso Vegetarian Refried Beans
Walnut Acres Maple and Onion Baked Beans

Canned Beans
Black Beans
Black Eye Peas
Cannellini (white kidney beans)
Fava Beans
Garbanzo Beans (chickpeas)
Northern Beans
Pinto Beans
Red Kidney Beans

Dried Beans (Hint: Use a pressure cooker for quick
    and easy cooking of dried beans.)
Baby Lima Beans
Black Beans
Black Eye Peas
Garbanzo Beans (chickpeas)
Great Northern Beans
Green Split Peas
Kidney Beans
Lentils
Lima Beans
Mixed Beans for Soups
Navy Beans
Northern Beans
Pinto Beans
Roman Beans
Yellow Split Peas

Frozen Side Dishes
Empire Kosher Potato Pancakes
French Fries (make sure there is no animal flavor or fat)
Gabila's Potato Knishes
Hashbrowns (make sure there is no animal flavor or fat)
Onion Rings (make sure there is no animal flavor, animal fat, or
    eggs)
Tater Tots (make sure there is no animal flavor or fat)
Vegetable and Pasta Combinations

Grains
Arrowhead Mills
        Amaranth
        Buckwheat Groats
        Bulgur Wheat
        Quinoa
        Whole Millet

Casbah
>Couscous
>Couscous, Lentil, Rice, or Spanish Pilaf
>Tabouli

Fantastic Foods
>Arborio Rice
>Basmati Rice
>Couscous and Organic Whole Wheat Couscous
>Four Grain Rice Pilaf
>Jasmine Rice
>Tabouli

Lundberg Family Farms
>Organic Arborio
>Organic California Brown Basmati
>Organic California Brown Jasmine
>Organic Short Grain Brown Rice
>Organic Sushi Rice
>Wild Rice Blend

Near East
>Couscous
>Lentil Pilaf
>Rice Pilaf
>Taboule Wheat Salad
>Wheat Pilaf

Old World
>Bulgur Wheat

Quaker
>Barley

Rice Select
>Jasmati, Kasmati, Risotto, Sushi, or Texmati Rice

Uncle Ben's
   Brown Rice

Wolff's
   Kasha

Instant Seasoned Rice
Mahatma One Step Dish
   Saffron Yellow Seasonings and Rice

Manischewitz
   Brown Rice Pilaf Mix
   Lentil Pilaf Mix
   Rice Pilaf Mix
   Spanish Pilaf Mix
   Wheat Pilaf Mix

Near East
   Long Grain and Wild Rice
   Spanish Rice Pilaf

Rice A Roni
   Original Long Grain and Wild Rice
   Spanish Rice

Rice Select
   Shiitake Mushroom Rice
   Smokey Cowboy Rice and Beans
   Sonoran Mexican Rice

Uncle Ben's
   Long Grain and Wild Rice Original Recipe

Canned Vegetables
Artichokes
Asparagus
Beets
Carrots
Collard Greens
Corn (regular and cream style)
Green Beans
Green Peas
Hearts of Palm
Hominy (grits)
Kale
Lima Beans
Mixed Vegetables
Mushrooms
Okra
Sauerkraut
Spinach
Succotash (lima beans and corn)
Sweet Peas
Sweet Potatoes
Tomatoes
Turnip Greens
Wax Beans
White Potatoes
Yams

Frozen Vegetables
Artichoke Hearts
Asparagus
Bell Peppers
Black Eye Peas
Broccoli
Brussels Sprouts
Carrots
Cauliflower

Collard Greens
Corn
Green Beans
Green Peas
Kale
Lima Beans
Mixed Vegetables
Mustard Greens
Okra
Onions
Peas and Carrots
Spinach
Squash
Succotash
Turnip Greens

SOUPS:

Amy's Organic Soups
- Low Fat Black Bean Vegetable
- Low Fat Butternut Squash
- Low Fat Minestrone
- Low Fat No Chicken Noodle
- Low Fat Split Pea
- Low Fat Vegetable Barley

Bean Cuisine (dry seasoned mixes found either near canned soups or dry beans)
- Island Black Bean
- Lots of Lentil Soup
- Santa Fe Corn Chowder
- Thick as Fog Split Pea
- 13 Bean Bouillabaisse
- Ultima Pasta e Fagioli
- White Bean Provencal

Dr. McDougall's (cups of soup/meals)
    Baked Ramen Noodle Soup
    Minestrone
    Pinto Beans and Rice
    Rice and Pasta Pilaf
    Split Pea with Barley Soup
    Tamale Pie
    Tortilla soup

Fantastic Foods (cups of soup/meals)
    Baja Black Bean Chipotle Soup
    Buckaroo Bean Chili Soup
    Green Onion Miso with Tofu Soup
    Split Pea Soup
    Tuscan Tomato and Shells Soup
    Sesame Miso Soup
    Summer Vegetable Rice Soup
    Vegetarian Chicken Noodle Soup

Fantastic Soup and Dip Recipe Mix
    Garlic Herb
    Onion

Health Valley
    Organic Black Bean Soup
    Organic Lentil Soup
    Organic Potato Leek Soup
    Organic Split Pea Soup
    Organic Tomato Soup

Health Valley Fat-Free
  5 Bean Vegetable
  14 Garden Vegetable

Health Valley Fat-Free or Lowfat (cups of soup/meals)
  Cantonese Rice
  Chili
  Garden Split Pea
  Lentil with Couscous
  Pasta Italiano
  Shiitake Rice
  Spicy Black Bean with Couscous
  Zesty Black Bean with Rice

Healthy Choice
  Country Vegetable
  Garden Vegetable

Imagine Organic
  Creamy Broccoli Soup
  Creamy Butternut Squash Soup
  Creamy Portobello Mushroom Soup
  Creamy Potato Leek Soup
  Creamy Sweet Corn Soup
  Creamy Tomato Soup

Lipton Recipe Soup Mix Recipe Secrets (powder)
  Onion
  Onion-Mushroom
  Vegetable

Pacific Foods All Natural Soup
    Cashew Carrot Ginger
    Creamy Butternut Squash
    Organic Mushroom Broth
    Organic Vegetable Broth

Progresso Soup
    Lentil

Westbrae Natural
    Alabama Black Bean Gumbo
    Great Plains Savory Bean
    Louisiana Bean Stew
    Mediterranean Lentil
    Old World Split Pea
    Santa Fe Vegetable
    Spicy Southwest Vegetable

GRAVY AND SAUCES:

Annie's
      Smokey Maple BBQ Sauce

Hain Pure Foods
      Vegetarian Brown Gravy Mix
      Vegetarian Chicken Flavored Gravy Mix

Hunt's
      Manwich Sloppy Joe Sauce

Loma Linda Fat Free Gravy Quik
      Vegetarian Brown Gravy Mix
      Vegetarian Chicken Style Gravy Mix
      Vegetarian Country Style Gravy Mix
      Vegetarian Mushroom Gravy Mix
      Vegetarian Onion Gravy Mix

SNACK ITEMS:

Cookies
Corn Chips
Dips
Dried Fruits (raisins, dates, prunes, figs, etc.)
Fruit Leather
Granola Bars
Nuts
Popcorn
Potato Chips (watch for lard in ingredients)
Pretzels
Rice Cakes
Salsa
Seeds (sunflower, pumpkin, etc.)
Trail Mix

Crackers

Carr's Table Water Crackers
- Original
- With Cracked Pepper
- With Roasted Garlic and Herbs
- With Toasted Sesame Seeds

Carr's Whole Wheat Crackers

Devonsheer Melba Toast and Melba Rounds
- Garlic
- Plain
- Rye
- Sesame
- Vegetable
- Wheat

Frookie Snack Crackers
- Wheat and Onion
- Wheat and Rye

Hol Grain Crackers
- Brown Rice A Light Touch of Salt
- Brown Rice No Salt
- Brown Rice Onion and Garlic

Keebler Club Partners
- Original
- Reduced Fat
- Reduced Sodium

Keebler Toasteds
>   Onion
>   Rye
>   Savory Crisps (multigrain and roasted garlic)
>   Sesame
>   Wheat

Keebler Townhouse Crackers
>   Classic
>   Reduced Fat

Keebler Zesta Saltine Crackers

Nabisco
>   Harvest Crisps—5 Grain
>   Harvest Crisps—Garden Vegetable
>   Low Sodium Ritz Crackers
>   Ritz Crackers
>   Ritz Crackers with Whole Wheat
>   Ritz Sticks
>   Soup and Oyster Crackers
>   Uneeda Biscuit
>   Waverly

Nabisco Premium Saltine Crackers
>   Fat Free
>   Low Sodium
>   Original
>   Unsalted Tops
>   With Multi-Grain

Nabisco Triscuit
   Deli Style Rye
   Garden Herb
   Low Sodium
   Original
   Reduced Fat
   Roasted Garlic
   Wheat N' Bran

Nabisco Wheat Thins
   Low Sodium
   Multi-Grain
   Original
   Reduced Fat

Ralston Saltines
   Original
   Unsalted Tops

Sunshine Krispy Original Saltine Crackers

Wasa
   Fiber Rye Crispbread
   Hearty Rye Crispbread
   Light Rye Crispbread
   Sourdough Rye Crispbread

DESERTS:

<u>Canned fruit</u>
Apples
Applesauce
Berries
Cherries
Citrus Fruit
Cranberry Sauce
Peaches
Pears
Pineapple

<u>Cookies</u>
Barbara's Bakery
      Blueberry Fig Bars
      Traditional Fig Bars
      Wheat Free Fig Bars
      Whole Wheat Fig Bars

Frookie All Natural
      Frookwich Chocolate
      Frookwich Vanilla
      Funky Monkeys Chocolate

Kedem Tea Biscuits
      Chocolate
      Plain
      Vanilla

Keebler Grahams
      Chocolate
      Cinnamon Crisp
      Original

Nabisco
> Golden Oreo
> Grahams—Original
> Mini Oreo
> Teddy Grahams—Cinnamon

Newman's Own Organics
> Alphabet Cookies (wheat-free/dairy-free)
> Fig Newmans (wheat-free/dairy-free)
> Newman's Ginger O's
> Newman's-O's (wheat-free/dairy-free)

Frozen Desserts
Marie Callender's
> Apple, Cherry Crunch, Dutch Apple, and Razzleberry Pie

Pepperidge Farms
> Apple and Raspberry Turnovers

TAKE-OUT FOODS:
The quickest way to prepare a meal is to take out food. Stop at your local deli counter and pick up potato salad, health salads, hummus, salsa, and other goodies. Ethnic fast food places are also good sources for a quick bite. You can purchase Mexican bean tacos or burritos, vegetable lo mein, and/or stir-fried vegetables. Chinese and Thai restaurants are usually happy to prepare any dish without meat if you politely ask. Be sure to request that they do not use fish sauce. Italian pizza and eggplant subs are also terrific items. Some restaurants still fry their food in lard, so you may want to ask some questions before ordering a meal.

Eating Out

Eating out is getting easier and easier for both vegetarians and vegans. If you have a choice, try an ethnic restaurant. Besides Chinese, Mexican, and Italian, good vegetarian eateries (especially in cities) include Indian, Middle Eastern, Thai, Ethiopian, Japanese, and Vietnamese. And, of course, even quick service restaurant chains and truck stops now offer salad bars or other vegetarian choices. For a list of vegetarian restaurants throughout the United States visit http://vrg.org/restaurant/ index.htm

TRUCK STOPS AND SHOPPING CENTERS:
The following is a list of some of the vegetarian items we've found in these places.

Salad Bars
Grits
Oatmeal
Hash Browns (make sure they are not fried in lard and do not
    contain bacon)
Waffles and Pancakes
English Muffins, Bagels, etc.
Salads
Vegetarian Soups
French Fries or Onion Rings (make sure they are not fried in
    animal fat)
Lettuce, Tomato, and Vegetable Sandwiches
Coleslaw
Eggplant Subs
Bean Burritos
Veggie Burgers
Side Orders of Vegetables (make sure they do not contain ham)
Pretzels

BOARDWALKS, CARNIVALS, PARKS, AND BALL PARKS:

Even these havens of typical Americana have items for the vegetarian or vegan. (Also see information on ballparks at http://www.soyhappy.org/venue.htm)

Sorbet or Italian Ices
French Fries and Onion Rings (make sure they are not fried in
    lard)
Pizza (can be ordered without cheese and with extra vegetables)
Fresh Fruit Cups
Pretzels with Mustard
Fruit Shakes
Funnel Cakes or Fried Dough
Corn on the Cob
French Fried Vegetables
Vegetable Subs
Popcorn

VEGETARIAN FOOD ON AIRLINES:

Today, to save money, many airlines no longer offer meals on domestic flights. However, if your flight does offer a meal and you require a special meal for reasons of health, religion, or personal preference, most airlines will accommodate your needs if you let them know at least 24 hours before your flight departs. We would recommend that you describe your food requirements when making your reservation and then remind the airline again 24 hours before your departure time.

Special meals available may include vegetarian with dairy, vegetarian without dairy or eggs (vegan), diabetic, low-fat, etc. Be specific about what you are requesting. Beware that a low-fat meal probably contains an animal product. Also, quite often airlines forget your special meal request. Therefore, it's best to bring along your own food (especially on long flights).

Vegetarian and Vegan Menu Items at Restaurant and Quick Service Chains

From The Vegetarian Resource Group

Some people keep strictly kosher and will never eat in a non-kosher restaurant. Likewise, some vegetarians will never dine in a non-vegetarian establishment since they can never be sure that an item is 100 percent vegetarian or vegan. However, most vegetarians eat out, and each person decides where to draw his or her line. We encourage restaurants to try to meet the needs of vegetarians and for vegetarians to do the best they can. Please realize that life isn't perfect, and mistakes can be made. If we want a better world, let's work together in a positive way so it will be easier for you to be vegetarian and for restaurants to offer vegetarian options.

PLEASE NOTE: We depend on company statements for product and ingredient information. It is impossible to be 100 percent sure about a statement, information can change, people have different views, and mistakes can be made. Please use your own best judgement about whether a product is suitable for you. To be certain, do further research or confirmation on your own. If you want to be 100 percent sure, we suggest you do not eat items from these establishments. If you are like the majority of Americans, please do the best you can.

The contents of this book and our other publications, including web information, are not intended to provide personal medical advice. Medical advice should be obtained from a qualified health professional.

Since the 1980s, The Vegetarian Resource Group periodically asks major fast food and quick-service, casual restaurant chains for the latest information regarding the ingredients in their menu items. We recently contacted established chains as well as some new ones for this article.

Several restaurants told us what patrons buy directly influences formulations, suppliers, and menu selections. Purchasing 'veggie-friendly' or vegetarian/vegan-customizable menu offerings when dining out helps to keep these dishes on the menus and increase the number of 'veggie-friendly' selections.

Not all menu items at every chain are mentioned in this report. We have listed foods and ingredients that may be of interest to vegetarians and/or vegans. For those menu offerings that we've indicated already contain eggs or milk, there may be ingredients present that come from other dairy sources (such as whey), but space does not permit a complete, detailed summary. We assume that the ingredient statements and other information provided to us by the chains are true, accurate, and complete. However, readers should be aware that changes may occur in ingredient formulations and suppliers at any time, so they should always consult the chains' websites, call customer service hotlines, or inquire at particular locations.

In some cases, restaurant chains tell us specific information about ingredients beyond what appears on their websites, and this information is contained in the entries. When The VRG does not have the information needed for us to properly classify an ingredient, we list it as coming from a "non-reported source." Readers should understand that, by this, we mean the ingredient may or may not be of animal, dairy, or egg origin.

If you see an unfamiliar ingredient listed here, you may consult The VRG's Guide to Food Ingredients for more information. The current edition is available for $6. Visit our website at <www.vrg.org> to purchase it or call The VRG at (410) 366-8343, 9 a.m. to 5 p.m. Eastern Time Monday through Friday. Also, look for updated entries to our Guide to Food Ingredients in our free e-mail newsletter to which readers may subscribe through our website at <www.vrg.org/vrgnews>.

PLEASE NOTE: Most restaurant chains are unsure whether the enzymes used in their cheeses are microbial- or animal-derived. Some chains said that typically the enzyme used is microbial, but they could not guarantee this because suppliers may use whatever enzyme is available. At this time, if a restaurant or food company in the United States calls their lacto-ovo food vegetarian, it may not guarantee that the cheese is made with vegetable rennet. If you are concerned about this, you should avoid items with cheese.

Many restaurant websites now list ingredients, with some being more complete than others. When you talk to a customer service representative or a quality assurance manager in a positive way about the sources of an ingredient, such as natural flavors or mono- and diglycerides, you are educating people about the concerns of vegetarians and vegans. You are also helping the next person who inquires about that ingredient, too. We have an interesting situation where a chain may offer an item from a company that manufactures products that vegetarians will eat at home. However, the chain may state they can not guarantee that any food they offer is vegetarian. This may be to protect the chain. Also, problems arise because some vegetarians will use a particular food while others won't, restaurants may not always use a separate cooking surface for meat and vegetarian foods, it is very easy to make a mistake in food service, etc. This approach of stating that the establishment has nothing vegetarian appears to warn the concerned vegetarian and protect the business, but it doesn't inform the vegetarian who wishes to eat out. We will be interested to see how restaurants and the vegetarian movement solve this problem.

Restaurants seem to want to further research the sources of their ingredients so as to serve better their vegetarian and vegan guests. Although these requests do not guarantee that restaurant chains will make changes in their ingredients or menus, they represent a first step toward this result. Some chains are testing vegetarian options in a few of their restaurants. If you are in any restaurant where a vegetarian or vegan option is being offered, showing your support and purchasing the food item is a way to keep vegetarian and vegan options on the menus or to put them there in the first place. Perhaps one day there will be many all-vegetarian or all-vegan national restaurant chains.

Please use this guide to restaurant chains only as a starting point, not as definite answers. Menus and ingredients do change, sometimes suddenly and without well-publicized notification. If you see information which you believe is incorrect, please let us know. Visit <www.vrg.org> for updates.

Definitions:

VEGETARIAN AND VEGAN
Vegetarian items do not contain meat, fish, or fowl. Vegan foods, in addition to being vegetarian, are free of all animal ingredients, including dairy products and eggs.

GELATIN
Gelatin can be made from cows, pigs, fish, and other animals. It is animal protein used especially for its thickening and gelling properties. It is often in candies. Kosher gelatin can be made with fish and/or beef. (Viewpoint, Vol 30, #4)

MONO- AND DIGLYCERIDES
Monoglycerides and diglycerides are common food additives used to blend certain ingredients together, such as oil and water, which would not otherwise blend well. They are often found in bakery products, beverages, ice cream, chewing gum, shortening, whipped toppings, margarine, and confections. The commercial source may be either animal (cow- or hog-derived) or vegetable, and they may be synthetically made as well. Archer Daniels Midland Co., a large manufacturer of monoglycerides, reported that they use soybean oil.

NATURAL FLAVORS

The definition of natural flavorings and flavors from 21CFR101.22 (the Code of Federal Regulations) is as follows:

"The term natural flavor or natural flavoring means the essential oil, oleoresin, essence or extractive, protein hydrolysate, distillate, or any product of roasting, heating or enzymolysis, which contains the flavoring constituents derived from a spice, fruit or fruit juice, vegetable or vegetable juice, edible yeast, herb, bark, bud, root, leaf or similar plant material, meat, seafood, poultry, eggs, dairy products, or fermentation products thereof, whose significant function in food is flavoring rather than nutritional."

In other words, natural flavors can be pretty much anything approved for use in food. It's nearly impossible to tell what is in natural flavors unless the company has specified it on the label. A few of the vegetarian- and vegan-oriented companies are doing this now, but the overwhelming majority of food manufacturers do not.

Why do companies "hide" ingredients under "natural flavors?" It's considered a way of preserving the product's identity and uniqueness. This is similar to thinking behind a "secret recipe." Company executives worry that someone would be able to duplicate their product if they publish what their products' flavorings were.

So, what is a vegetarian to do? Call the company. Ask them what's in the flavorings. They may not be able to tell you, but the more they hear this question, the more likely they are to become concerned about putting a clarifying statement on their labels. It does work in some cases (such as when a significant number of people wrote to the USDA about standardizing the qualities necessary for a product to be classified as organic), although it may take awhile. We have already had several large food companies contact us about their natural flavors and how to word their labels if they use only vegetarian or vegan flavorings. They called because it had come to their attention that this was a concern for vegetarians and vegans.

RENNET
Typically, cheese is made by coagulating cow or goat's milk with rennet or rennin (an enzyme). Traditionally, rennet was from a calf's stomach. There are also cheeses, which are made with vegetable or microbial enzymes (rennet). In most non-vegetarian restaurant in the United States, it's unlikely restaurant staff will know what kind of cheese is being used.

SUGAR
Some food ingredients may have been processed through the use of animal, egg, or dairy products. Sugar, for instance, may have been filtered through cow bone char. See Vegetarian Journal, Issue 4, 2007. Currently, there is not a way to be sure about the source of sugar, so we are not labeling it as an animal ingredient. Note that organic sugar is not processed with bone char.

A NOTE ABOUT EATING OUT AND SUPPORTING VEGETARIAN RESTAURANTS
Be aware that you can never be '100% safe' when eating out. Some readers may feel more secure in restaurants that focus on vegetarian foods. See The Vegetarian Resource Group's website at <www.vrg.org> for a list of more than 2,000 vegetarian and vegetarian-friendly restaurants in the United States and Canada.

Remember: Please use this guide to restaurant chains only as a starting point, not as definite answers. Menus and ingredients do change, sometimes suddenly and without well-publicized notification. If you see information you believe is incorrect, please let us know.

APPLEBEE'S: When we first contacted Applebee's, the leading fast-casual restaurant chain, in early 2007 for this update, they sent us a list of 'vegetarian' menu items upon request. They referred to these as entrées that "can be made meatless or are meatless already: Chicken & Broccoli Pasta Alfredo, Chicken Fajita Roll-Up, Nachos Nuevos, Mozzarella Sticks, Veggie Patch Pizza, and Vegetable Fajitas con Sizzle."

When The VRG inquired further about these items, we were told that entrée ingredients and preparation techniques vary widely from location to location and so no generalizations are possible. We received the following statement: "There are no dedicated fryers; potato items can be fried with meat items. There are protocols for sanitizing grill surfaces [but Applebee's cannot assure against cross-contamination]."

Applebee's sent us this disclaimer in March 2007: "Applebee's International, Inc., does not claim its products to be vegetarian, to meet the requirements for a vegetarian diet, or to meet the criteria for any other special dietary regimen. Dairy and egg products may be present in meatless recipes. Trace amounts of meat or animal products may be present as a result of preparation or cooking."

Of the menu items listed above, only the Vegetable Fajitas con Sizzle appears to be free of animal ingredients. The sauce is soy-based, and the tortilla is milk-free. Sour cream and cheese can be omitted. We could not get further information on how the vegetables are prepared in this menu item. Mexi-Rice, which contains no dairy or egg products, may accompany this entrée if requested; however, it is unknown if a meat-based stock is used in the rice.

BAJA FRESH: Baja Fresh is a chain of Mexican restaurants that opened in 1990 and now has close to 300 locations in more than 20 states. In October 2007, we spoke with Gloria Mendez, a Customer Relations Specialist at Baja Fresh.

Mendez told us that Baja Fresh does not provide a separate vegan menu. They do state on their website that they would be happy, upon request, to customize any menu item by omitting certain ingredients. This applies for in-house dining as well as their party packs.

She assured us that "there are no animal products in the preparation of our rice or beans; however, when we plate the beans on some entrées, they are sprinkled with cotija cheese that is made with animal rennet. The cotija cheese can be eliminated upon request." According to Mendez, the anejo cheese served at Baja Fresh also contains animal rennet, although the jack and cheddar cheeses, as stated in the manufacturer ingredient specifications, do not.

With the exception of the tortilla soup, which has a chicken base, Mendez said, "We do not use any other type of chicken or beef broth." There is no carmine in any menu item at Baja Fresh.

Based on standard product formulations, Mendez told us that the ranch dressing and the mayonnaise contain eggs. (The ranch dressing also contains butter.) The sour cream, flour tortillas, and the Salsa Crema contain milk or whey. The flour tortilla also contains L-cysteine, but Mendez did not specify its source. The corn tortilla does not contain L-cysteine and appears free of all animal ingredients. The guacamole and the sour cream do not contain gelatin.

Baja Fresh offers a 'Bare Style' burrito in a bowl without the tortilla. There is also a Grilled Veggie Burrito consisting of a blend of grilled peppers, chilies, and onions, layered with freshly simmered black or pinto beans, melted jack and cheddar cheese, lettuce, pico de gallo, and sour cream. Patrons may custom order either of these dishes to be free of animal products.

Other all-vegetable possibilities include customized nacho dishes with beans, guacamole, lettuce, and selected salsas. The side salad may be customized without the cheese. The rice side dish is free of animal ingredients.

Mendez emphasized that "variations [in ingredients] may occur due to differences in suppliers, ingredient substitutions, recipe revisions, or product assembly at the restaurant level. Baja Fresh does not assume responsibility for a patron's particular food sensitivity and encourages anyone with food sensitivities or special dietary needs to consult with a medical professional."

BURGER KING: In December 2006, Burger King declined our request for information regarding food ingredients in their menu items. This entry on Burger King is based on information published on the Burger King website that we read in October 2007.

Burger King offers a BK Veggie® Burger. The current ingredient statement on the Burger King website specifies, "This is NOT a vegan product." (Capitalization is Burger King's). The BK Veggie® Burger contains egg whites as well as dairy-derived calcium caseinate. The natural flavors are listed as being derived from "non-meat sources." The nutrition page at the Burger King website contains a footnote on the Veggie Burger stating, "Burger King Corporation makes no claim that the BK Veggie® Burger or any other of its other products meets the requirements of a vegetarian or vegan diet. The patty is cooked in the microwave." No further information is given except that it may be ordered with or without cheese or with or without mayonnaise.

Burger King restaurants in other countries also offer the BK Veggie® Burger (and other menu items not offered in the United States that appear to be appropriate for those choosing a meatless diet). Vegetarian travelers should check with the particular restaurant or the Burger King website to find out ingredient information.

Burger King states that it will customize any menu item according to a customer's tastes. However, Burger King has a disclaimer on its website about food ingredients. It states that it cannot be held responsible for a person's sensitivity to any food item. The disclaimer also specifies that variations in ingredient formulations may occur depending on supplier and on product assembly on a restaurant-by-restaurant basis.

According to the Burger King website, the French fries appear to contain no animal products and are fried in their own dedicated fryers using vegetable shortening. The Onion Rings, Hash Browns, French Toast Rounds and Sticks, and Cheesy

Tots™ are fried in fryers used to prepare meat-containing menu items. The Onion Rings contain grill flavor of a non-reported source. The Hash Browns contain mono- and diglycerides of a non-reported source. Sugar is listed as an ingredient in French Toast Sticks and in the Onion Rings.

In June 2007, the writer called the consumer relations line at Burger King about the L-cysteine in the sesame bun and the Cini-minis™. She was told that Burger King "cannot guarantee" the source of L-cysteine in its products. Previously, in March 2007, the writer was informed by another consumer representative at Burger King that the L-cysteine was not derived from human hair. In October 2007, the writer noticed that Burger King has placed the phrase "does not contain animal ingredients" at the end of its ingredient statements for each of its three buns.

Breakfast Foods

The Breakfast Syrup contains animal-derived natural flavors. The Biscuit, Croissan'wich™ croissant, Cheesy Tots™, and Cini-minis™ contain eggs and/or dairy. The Vanilla Icing on the Cini-minis™ contains natural flavors of a non-reported source. The Mott's® Strawberry Flavored Applesauce is listed as containing sugar and natural flavors of non-reported sources. The grape and strawberry jams appear free of animal ingredients. They do contain sugar.

Desserts/Beverages

The Dutch Apple Pie contains sugar and mono- and diglycerides of a non-reported source. The 'artificial flavors' (as 'natural flavors' are not listed) in the Pie are listed as coming from "plant sources." Minute Maid® Orange Juice and Minute Maid® Apple Juice appear free of animal ingredients.

CHIPOTLE

Chipotle Mexican Grill opened its doors in 1993 and now has almost 100 locations in 27 states. Chipotle, called "the fast food equivalent of Whole Foods Market" by the Pittsburgh Post-Gazette in 2007, is a leader among fast casual restaurant chains in terms of offering what it calls "Food with Integrity." This philosophy of food refers to foods that are "...unprocessed, seasonal, family-farmed, sustainable, nutritious, naturally raised, added-hormone free, organic, or artisanal."

The chain also helps to establish sustainable practices in produce farming (such as avocados and lettuce thus far). As of late 2007, a quarter of Chipotle's beans were organic, and their goal is to use only organic beans in all of their restaurants. As of late 2007 when this article was written, Chipotle had recycling containers in 70 percent of their restaurants.

Chipotle's website is very vegetarian-friendly in that it states which menu items are vegetarian. They also specifically address what vegans and vegetarians may eat at their restaurants, thereby indicating that this chain does recognize the difference between vegetarians and vegans and can make both groups happy! Almost all items can be custom-ordered at Chipotle to make menu items animal-free. In October 2007, we spoke with Joe Stupp of Chipotle, and he helped clarify questions about their offerings.

Stupp told us that Chipotle does not use animal rennet in any of its cheeses, using a "vegetable-based rennet" instead. The guacamole does not contain gelatin nor dairy. There is no L-cysteine in any of its bread products. The black beans "...are completely animal-free, but the pinto beans are prepared with bacon." The sour cream contains no gelatin. There is no carmine in any of its salsas. There is no added sugar in Chipotle menu items except in the pinto beans.

Stupp elaborated on the three basic types of foods at Chipotle: burritos, tacos, and salads. The burritos consist of a flour tortilla, cilantro-lime rice, choice of pinto or vegetarian black beans, meat, salsa, cheese or sour cream, and romaine lettuce. The rice at Chipotle is free of animal ingredients. The vegetarian burrito includes guacamole rather than meat. The fajita burrito is just like a burrito but with sautéed peppers and onions instead of beans. The vegetarian fajita has both sautéed veggies and vegetarian black beans instead of meat and includes guacamole. Patrons can also get a burrito or fajita in a bowl with everything listed here except the tortilla.

The tacos may include either a soft flour tortilla or a crispy corn shell, choice of meat, salsa, cheese or sour cream, and romaine lettuce. The crispy corn shell is free of all animal ingredients. Patrons may customize the tacos, as well as the burritos and salads, as they wish.

The salads at Chipotle consist of romaine lettuce with choice of beans, meat, salsa, and cheese, with freshly made chipotle-honey vinaigrette (which does contain honey).

The 'vegetarian' option at Chipotle (listed after their meat options on the menu) includes the freshly made guacamole and vegetarian black beans in either burrito, taco, or salad style. Sautéed peppers and onions may be added to make a vegetarian fajita.

DOMINO'S: Pizza ingredients at Domino's have not changed significantly since our last Guide to Fast Food and Quick Service Chains was published. We spoke with Clay Harvey of the Customer Service Department at Domino's about the ingredients in their menu items. He told us that the enzymes in Domino's cheeses are not animal-derived. Likewise, the enzymes in all of the pizza doughs are non-animal-derived.

Domino's Pizza Sauce remains free of animal ingredients, although it contains sugar. The Thin Crust at Domino's is free of animal ingredients. The Hand-Tossed Crust contains whey and L-cysteine of a non-animal source. The Deep Dish Crust contains several dairy products, as well as natural flavors and mono-and diglycerides of non-reported sources.

The Garlic Dipping Sauce appears free of animal ingredients. The Marinara Dipping Sauce contains natural flavors of non-reported sources and sugar.

Domino's offers salads that can be customized to suit vegetarians and vegans. For example, Domino's told us that the Garden Salad may be purchased without the cheese. The Golden Italian Dressing and the Light Italian Dressing appear to be free of animal ingredients. All of the other salad dressings at Domino's contain fish, eggs, and/or dairy.

The 'butter base 20' and 'natural butter flavor' listed in Domino's Deep Dish Crust are vegetable oil-derived. The banana and jalapeño peppers are listed as containing natural flavors and polysorbate 80 of non-reported sources.

We asked about all of the natural flavors in Domino's products, but Domino's was unable to give The VRG any information about them. Harvey said, "Domino's does not specify the source of the [natural] flavors used in our products. It would require a great deal of time to research."

When asked about the source of the L-cysteine in several of its products, Harvey told us that L-cysteine is "non-animal derived" in its Hand-Tossed Crust, the Breadsticks, the Cheesy Bread, and the Cinna Stix. The Breadsticks and Cinna Stix contain whey and natural flavors of non-reported sources. The Cheesy Bread contains cheese and other milk products in addition to natural flavors of non-reported sources. The Sweet Icing Dipping Cup used with the Cinna Stix contains mono- and diglycerides of a non-reported source.

The Oreo® Thin Dessert Style Crust contains natural flavors of a non-reported source. The Vanilla Sauce contains sugar, polysorbate 60, and natural flavors of non-reported sources. The White Icing is listed as having mono- and diglycerides and natural flavors, also of non-reported sources.

FRESH CHOICE (California, Texas, Washington)
LIST OF MENU ITEMS CALLED "VEGETARIAN VEGAN" BY FRESH CHOICE:

Specialty Salads: Cool Napa Crunch, Fuji Apple & Papaya Washabi Toss Spinach Dijon, Strawberry Fields Spinach, Winter Mixed Greens w/ Maple Orange Vinaigrette

Prepared Salads: Asian Broccoli Slaw, Asian Edamame & Pasta, Asian Slaw (Fat-Free), Black Bean Fresca, Chili-Lime Fiesta Bean (Low-Fat), Chipotle Hummus, Creamy Dijon Potato (Fat-Free), Creole Corn & Black-Eyed Pea, Crisp Apple Pineapple (Fat-Free), Crunchy Quinoa, Edamame & Black-Eyed Peas, Fresh Hot Smokey Salsa (Low-Fat), Fresh Vegetable Medley, Ginger Soy Long, Italian Tomato & Cucumber (Fat-Free), Italian Vegetable Medley (Low-Fat), Jicama Citrus (Low-Fat), Jumpin' Beans (Low-Fat), Lemon Garlic Pasta (Low-Fat), Madras Curried Rice (Low-Fat), Marinated Cucumber (Fat-Free), Marinated Sesame Cucumber (Low-Fat), Moroccan Lentil, No Fry Stir Fry Rice, Roasted Garlic Basil Potato, Roasted Vegetable, Salsa Fresca (Fat-Free), Summer Garden Pasta (Fat-Free), Tabbouleh, Thai Shredded Slaw (Low-Fat), Toasted Couscous w/Garden Vegetables, Wild Rice & Cranberry, Zesty Cucumber & Tomato

Prepared Seasonal Vegetables: Balsamic Oven-Roasted Vegetables, Corn (Low-Fat), Fresh Summer Italian Bruschetta, Ginger Roasted Sesame Carrots, Pineapple Papaya Salsa (Fat-Free), Roasted Yukon Gold Potato, Squash Ratatouille (Fat-Free)

Soups: Black Beans Sante Fe (Low-Fat), Carrot Ginger (Fat-Free), Confetti Bean Chili, (Low-Fat), Garden Bean Stew (Low-Fat), Greek Artichoke & Lemon Rice (Low-Fat), Harvest Vegetable (Fat-Free), Hearty Garden Vegetable Barley (Low-Fat), Hearty Vegetable (Fat-Free), Mushroom Bean & Barley (Low-Fat), Pho Noodle Bowl (Low-Fat), Ratatouille Stew (Fat-Free), Red Bean Chili (Low-Fat), Roasted Vegetable & Butternut Squash Medley (Low-Fat), Rustic Country Vegetable (Low-Fat), Savory Bean (Low-Fat), Southern Lentil (Low-Fat), Spicy Vegetable Gumbo (Low-Fat), Summer Squash (Fat-Free), Thai Coconut Ginger, Tomato Basil Florentine (Fat-Free), Tuscan White Bean & Vegetable (Low-Fat), Vegetable Barley (Fat-Free), Vegetable Minestrone (Low-Fat), Vegetarian Vegetable (Fat-Free)

Pasta & Rice: Asian Vegetable Medley (Fat-Free), Baked Potato (Fat-Free), Pomodoro Sauce (Fat-Free), Spicy Thai Noodles w/ Marinated Tofu (Low-Fat); Peking Rice, Vegetarian Jambalaya (Low-Fat), White Rice (Fat-Free).

Tofu is also on the salad bar. Not every item will be at a restaurant.

Fresh Choice said they don't claim to be a vegetarian restaurant, but a salad bar is conducive to offering many vegetarian items. They use the term vegetarian since it's commonly understood by the general population. The words appear on signage above the dishes. The ingredient statements are also posted above the dishes.

There is no meat in vegetarian items but there could be eggs and dairy. Vegan items do not contain meat, eggs, or dairy. There is animal rennet in cheeses (especially cheddar, Jack, and mozzarella) and that's why there is no vegetarian pizza. They said if their cheeses contain animal rennet, they will not label the item vegetarian.

All store locations have their own listing on the website and those are the most current menus. Texas and Washington have their own menus that are different from California's.

There is no designated place in the kitchen just for vegetarian/vegan preparation apart from meat products, but there is proper sanitation between uses. Something used for chicken one day could be used for vegetables the next day. They do not have color-coded utensils.

Fresh Choice has a fifty-foot salad bar and a soup arcade. A spokesperson said the word "vegetarian" was used since the beginning almost twenty years ago. At that time, they had tabouli and couscous salads but they weren't very popular. Now, since conventional stores have made them popular and have educated the public about them, Fresh Choice is offering them more and more. The term "vegan" was introduced maybe fifteen years ago. Fresh Choice said that "vegans are the most vocal" to Fresh Choice about what they want in a restaurant and they have tried to meet their requests and expectations. Now they are selling more locally grown and local organic produce as fresh and in prepared salads. However, because organic laws are so strict as to how organic foods must be displayed especially when sold next to non-organic foods, it would be difficult to market the foods as "organic" and it would be cost-prohibitive to convert totally to organic. They are exploring adding more vegan items. Since we started looking at their list we noticed several "new" vegan dishes with quinoa and couscous on the menu.

McDONALD'S: McDonald's states that it makes no claims about its food items being vegetarian or vegan: "No products are certified as vegetarian; all products may contain trace amounts of ingredients derived from animals. If you wish further information or have special sensitivities or dietary concerns regarding specific ingredients in specific menu items, please call us."

This fast food chain also states that it will "gladly accommodate customer requests to custom-order items without meat.... Note that even though we provide the flexibility to order items without meat, we cannot guarantee that during preparation the item does not come into contact with meat or poultry."

Although McDonald's has tested veggie burgers in the recent past, there are none that are currently offered. McDonald's states, "After testing several types of veggie hamburgers in different parts of the country, we've chosen not to offer one on our national menu at this time.... Ultimately, however, it's our customers who choose what's on our menu. We'll continue to offer those menu items that are most popular with a majority of our customers."

When we inquired about certain menu items in late 2006, McDonald's told us that it is possible to order just a bun with certain condiments. However, it is most likely not possible to order a customized salad (for example, without the bacon bits) since salad preparation occurs in the morning. Restaurant patrons are encouraged to inquire at particular McDonald's restaurants if they wish to order a customized menu item.

McDonald's told us that the enzymes in the American and shredded Parmesan cheeses were animal-derived. We were also told that the L-cysteine in the Honey Wheat Roll and the Baked Apple Pie was also animal-derived, specifically from duck feathers. Concerning the microingredients that are currently vegetable-derived, McDonald's emphasized that "...although we have confirmed these sources with our current suppliers' formulas, we cannot guarantee that these ingredients will remain of vegetable sources in the future."

In July 2007, 'kosher gelatin' was listed as an ingredient in the yogurt of the Fruit 'n Yogurt Parfait and the Fruit and Walnut Salad served at McDonald's. In late August 2007, the writer was told that the gelatin was "from an animal source" and that the natural flavors in the yogurt were animal-derived.

The information below was taken from the McDonald's website Ingredient Statement:

Other Breakfast Foods
The Biscuits are made with milk. The Hash Browns are listed as containing "natural beef flavor" that is further described as containing milk. All other breakfast foods, except the English muffin, contain eggs or dairy. The Low-Fat Granola contains honey and sugar. The Whipped Margarine contains whey.

Other Lunch/Dinner Foods
All of the salad dressings, burger sauces, and nugget sauces contain animal ingredients, eggs, dairy, and/or ingredients of non-reported sources except the Sweet 'n Sour Sauce, Newman's Own® Low Fat Balsamic Vinaigrette, and Newman's Own® Low Fat Sesame Ginger Dressing. The Butter Garlic Croutons contain dairy. The Big Mac®, regular, and sesame seed buns appear to be free of animal ingredients, although they do contain sodium stearoyl lactylate of a non-reported source. The Snack Wrap® tortilla contains sugar. The Chili Lime Tortilla Strips contain sugar. The Southwest Vegetable Blend appears free of animal ingredients.

Desserts and Beverages

The Baked Apple Pie contains L-cysteine of an animal source. The Cinnamon Melts contain eggs and dairy as well as sodium stearoyl lactylate and polysorbate 60, both of non-reported sources. The Apple Dippers appear to be free of animal ingredients. The plain McDonaldland® Cookies appear to be all-vegetable, too, although they contain sugar. All other cookies, including the Sugar Cookie, contain eggs and dairy. The Minute Maid® Apple Juice Box and orange juice appear to be free of animal ingredients.

MOE'S SOUTHWEST GRILL: (Scattered through about 20 states. Not California or Northwest)
MENU ITEMS AT MOE'S THAT ARE NOTED AS VEGETARIAN BY THE CHAIN: Art Vandalay Burrito, Unanimous Decision Taco, Instant Friend Quesadilla, Super Kingpin Quesadilla, Personal Trainer Salad, Ruprict Nachos

This report is based on information from the R&D Department at Moe's. All foods at Moe's labeled vegetarian are customizable. This means that the menu items can be ordered without one or more components. TOFU is not listed in the items specifically labeled as "vegetarian." It can be included in any menu item upon request and substituted for any meat product.

All burritos, tacos, and quesadillas come with patron's choice of black or pinto beans. Moe's stated that the beans and rice contain no animal products and they are prepared separately from meat products. The rice at Moe's is made with vegetable stock. The sautéed vegetables are prepared on a grill separate from meat products. The tofu is prepared on the same grill as the vegetables. The tofu does not contain any animal products but it is marinated in the "steak marinade," which does not contain any meat products.

Animal rennet is not used in any of the cheeses at Moe's and there is no gelatin used in either the guacamole or the sour cream. None of the salsas or sauces at Moe's contains animal ingredients. Moe's R&D said that none of the bread products, including the chips, contains animal-derived ingredients. However, since their pans are on a "line" the chain can't control cross-contamination by patrons (i.e., drippings of ingredients into other pans as people are serving themselves).

NOODLES & COMPANY: (Scattered through about 17 states)
MENU ITEMS CALLED VEGETARIAN BY NOODLES AND COMPANY WHEN ASKED: Japanese Pan Noodles (with vegetables), Bangkok Curry, Indonesian Peanut Sauté, Thai Curry Soup, Chinese Chop Salad, Penne Rosa, Whole Grain Tuscan Linguine (cheese omitted), Buttered Noodles (cheese omitted), House Marinara (cheese omitted)

Organic tofu may be added to any dish, Vegetable broth is used to sauté vegetables and tofu.

Their executive chef identified himself as a vegetarian and said he wanted to start a restaurant where he and his family could eat vegetarian meals. Noodles said they do not make any claims to being vegan or having vegan dishes "because of the controversy amongst the vegan community around the use of certain ingredients like sugar." They do not label specific dishes "vegetarian."

Their Mushroom Stroganoff and The Med Salad both contained sour cream with gelatin in it. They were actually making adjustments to their recipes now to include vegetarian sour cream. All of their restaurants should be providing the vegetarian version in the future. Their Pad Thai contains fish sauce and oyster sauce. Cheese may or may not contain animal rennet because not enough customers have voiced a preference. Cheese can be omitted from most dishes, though not the pesto. The Asparagus Linguine is a seasonal offering that can be ordered without the cheese. The sauce contains dairy and wine.

Each dish is custom made to order, when ordered. This "means that each dish is prepared specifically for each guest in its respective bowl or sauté pan. All of the chicken is seared on a flat top grill, separate from other meats and the tofu is tossed into a sauté pan when added to a noodle dish, soup, or salad."

PAPA JOHN'S: The VRG requested specific ingredient information from Papa John's in July 2007. In response, we were sent an updated Product Ingredients List (not available on the chain's website) and told they were researching answers. As of this writing, we have not heard back. Consequently, information contained in this entry is taken from the Papa John's website and its Ingredient Statement.

We noticed a significant change in Papa John's products since our last Fast Food Guide was published. Papa John's has removed all animal-derived rennet from their menu items. According to the Papa John's website, the cheeses are made with Chymax, a biosynthesized enzyme.

This FAQ question and answer about enzymes appears on the Papa John's website: "Do any of your products contain animal-derived enzymes? No. These enzymes are biosynthesized and/or vegetable derived enzymes—not animal." This FAQ does not explicitly state that the enzymes in some of their bread products are not animal-derived. For example, the Pan Pizza Shell is listed as having 'enzymes.' (This item also contains L-cysteine of a non-reported source.) Another change from our last update is the addition of milk-derived natural flavors to their thin crust pizza dough. The 'Pizza Dough' listed in the Papa John's Ingredients Statement appears to be free of animal ingredients. In the Ingredients Statement, the 'enzymes' listed for the Pizza Dough are from fungal or bacterial sources.

The Pizza Sauce and the Pizza Sauce Dipping Cup appear to be vegetable-based. The Robusto Pizza Sauce, which according to the Ingredients Statement is used primarily on the Pan Pizza, is listed as containing natural flavors and Asiago cheese flavor of non-reported sources. The Alfredo Sauce contains several dairy ingredients and natural flavors of non-reported sources. The Spinach Alfredo Sauce is made with several dairy products and mono- and diglycerides of non-reported sources. At the end of the Spinach Alfredo Sauce entry in the Ingredients Statement, it states that this "product does not contain animal rennet."

At the end of the entry for the Garlic Sauce, it states, "All ingredients are derived from vegetable, chemical, or natural sources or are synthesized from food grade ingredients—NO animal derivatives. Lactic acid is NOT considered dairy since it has been fermented." The source of the lactic acid was not given. The Seasoned Garlic Parmesan Sauce, which according to the Ingredients Statement may be used on the Seasoned Breadsticks, contains milk products and natural flavors of non-reported sources. The Special Seasoning packet also contains natural flavors of non-reported sources.

The crisp topping used on the Breakfast Pizza contains milk. The Cinnamon Apples and the Bumbleberry Filling contain sugar. The white icing is listed as containing stearic acid and natural flavors of non-reported sources. The Cinnamon Spread contains mono- and diglycerides of a non-reported source and sugar. The Caramel Sauce used in the Sweetreats is made with eggs.

The Italian Dressing at Papa John's is made with egg and milk products and contains natural flavors of a non-reported source.

PEI WEI: (About 77 restaurants)
MENU ITEMS AT PEI WEI THAT ARE NOTED AS VEGETARIAN BY THE CHAIN ON ITS MENU: Edamame, Pei Wei Spring Rolls; Blazing Noodles, Soba Miso Rice Bowl, Teriyaki Bowl, Thai Dynamite Signature Dish, Honey Seared Signature Dish, Spicy Korean Signataure Dish, Sweet & Sour Signature Dish. Rice is prepared separately from all other foods and is animal ingredient-free. Menu states the dishes that are vegetarian when ordered with tofu and vegetables.

Note: Their vegetarian items have a vegetarian icon next to the dish. If it doesn't have an icon, assume the dish contains an animal-derived ingredient, for example shrimp paste.

The Pad Thai is not listed as "vegetarian" although it does not contain meat, fish, or fowl when purchased as is. It is not listed since it has egg. Pei Wei does not use the word vegan on their menu since cookware could be used for meat one day, but tofu the next day. Of course cookware is washed and sanitized.

P.F. CHANG'S: (About 131 stores)
MENU ITEMS LABELED AS VEGETARIAN BY THE CHAIN:
Chang's Vegetarian Lettuce Wraps, Harvest Spring Rolls;
Buddha's Feast (steamed), Buddha's Feast (stir-fried), Coconut
Curry Vegetables, Stir-in Fried Eggplant, Vegetarian Ma Po Tofu,
Vegetable Chow Fun; Garlic Snap Peas, Shanghai Cucumber,
Sichuan-Style Asparagus, Spicy Green Beans, Spinach Stir-Fried
with Garlic

All entrées are served with a choice of steamed brown or white
rice. P.F. Chang's defines "vegetarian" as containing no animal
products, no egg, or dairy. They said they are stricter than most
in their definition. Since there are "shades of gray" in the
definitions of vegetarian and vegan, they wanted to keep it
simple for everyone, so they just use the word vegetarian. They
use white sugar and don't claim to be vegan. Their woks are
cleaned between uses. There are color-coded cutting boards to
keep meat separate from vegetables as well as separate
cleavers. There are separate areas in the kitchen for each food.
The food is served "in a line" in the stores. There are four to five
woks in a line. The line now contains all vegetable broth.

Tofu is prepared as a vegetable in either vegetable stock or
vegetable oil with nothing added that is non-vegetable. However,
you could request tofu for meat dishes. The rice is prepared
separately from all meat products with nothing non-vegetable
added.

Their vegetable dumplings (steamed and pan-fried) contain
egg and are not listed as "vegetarian" for this reason. The Lo
Mein Vegetable contains animal products. They are working on a
vegetarian sauce for a vegetarian lo mein, chow mein, and pan-
fried noodle dish. They use mushroom oyster sauces in their
dishes, but this is vegetarian. About 40% of their non-vegetarian
entrées have a chicken base. They can substitute crispy silken
tofu for five-spice bean curd (and vice versa) in any dish when
requested. P.F. Chang's said the five-spice bean curd is firmer
and has more flavor than the silken tofu. The chain states they are

flexible and strive to accommodate everyone and customize dishes made to order.

PIZZA HUT: Pizza Hut, the leading fast food chain that offers pizza, is a favorite restaurant for some vegetarians. For a previous Fast Food Guide, Pizza Hut chose not to participate and we could report only what they published on their website. However, throughout 2007, The VRG received some information by phone and e-mail from Amber MacZura, a Quality Assurance Specialist at Pizza Hut, Inc. We also referred to the Pizza Hut Ingredient Statement posted on the chain's website. Readers may note that this statement reads in part: "Although this data is based on standard portion product guidelines, variations can be expected due to seasonal influences, minor differences in product assembly per restaurant, and other factors.... Product data is based on current formulations as of date of posting." When we last checked the Ingredients Statement, it was reported current as of October 2006.

MacZura confirmed for us that the "enzymes in all of the doughs and cheeses are non-animal-derived." She also said, "The Pizza Cheese and String Cheese (used in the Stuffed Crust Pizza) ingredients are not of animal sources other than the milk itself."

MacZura explained that the "same bread dough is used in breadsticks and pizza, but the garlic bread dough is different." The garlic bread contains L-cysteine that MacZura reports is "animal-derived," but she could not indicate for us its specific animal source. The mono- and diglycerides in all the Pizza Hut bread products are vegetable-derived, coming from soy oil.

Here are more specifics on the many pizza doughs at Pizza Hut: The Thin 'N Crispy® Dough, the Hand-Tossed Style Dough, and the Stuffed Crust Dough appear to be free of animal products. The XL Full House™ Dough, the Bistro Dough, and the 4ForAll® are as well, but they contain sugar. The Bigfoot Dough Blend contains a dairy blend. The Pan Pizza and Personal Pan Pizza doughs contain whey. The Sicilian Dough is listed as having natural flavors of a non-reported source.

The Regular Pizza Sauce and the Sweet Pizza Sauce appear free of animal ingredients. The White Pizza Sauce contains both egg and dairy products. The Taco Bean Sauce is listed as having 'beef flavor,' although it does not appear to be made from beef.

The onion rings contain whey and the Jalapeño Poppers® contain whey and egg whites. The natural flavors in the onion rings, Jalapeño Poppers®, breadsticks, and the cheese breadsticks "are all vegetable-based flavors except [that] the cheese sticks do have one flavor that is milk-derived." MacZura also stated that the breadsticks and onion rings "are baked separately from any animal products." She pointed out, however, if a particular restaurant has 'Wing Street' brand chicken wings, the onion rings could be fried in the same oil as the chicken wings. Patrons can request that they be baked in an oven.

Readers may note that all appetizers at Pizza Hut contain whey, and, in some cases, other dairy-, egg-, or animal-derived ingredients. The Marinara Dipping Sauce used with many appetizers contains cheese. The Dulce de Leche Caramel Dipping Sauce contains several dairy products. The Garlic Herb Spread contains eggs.

Pizza Hut offers an optional Parmesan Parsley Blend packet made with non-animal-derived enzyme in the Parmesan cheese. MacZura told us that it "may be on some pizzas around the crust in some Limited Time Offers, but it would be labeled as such." Patrons can always ask that their pizza be made without it.

The Pasta Bakes® Marinara served at Pizza Hut appears to be all-vegetable with the exception of the white sauce, which contains a chicken base. This dish can be ordered without the white sauce.

The Pasta Bake Primavera can also be ordered without the white sauce. The rotelli and the Veggie Medley of these dishes appear free of animal ingredients. The spaghetti served at Pizza Hut, except that on the Bistro Menu, is free of animal ingredients.

The salads at Pizza Hut are made upon order, and cheese may be omitted. There are several salad dressings served at Pizza Hut, and many are free of animal ingredients, such as the French and Italian Dressings. High fructose corn syrup is used as the sweetener in these two dressings. MacZura told us that the natural flavors in these two dressings are "non-animal derived." The Light Italian Vinaigrette Dressing, the Vinaigrette Dressing, and the Light Italian Dressing also appear free of animal ingredients. The Balsamic and Basil Vinaigrette is listed as containing honey as well as white wine. The natural flavors in the other dressings mentioned in this paragraph are derived from non-animal sources, according to MacZura. All other dressings served at Pizza Hut, not mentioned here, contain animal products, eggs, and/or dairy.

Both the Apple Dessert Pizza and the Cherry Dessert Pizza contain dairy ingredients. MacZura confirmed for us that the Apple Topping natural flavors "are all from apples (apple essence)." The Cinnamon Sticks also contain dairy ingredients.

Selected Pizza Hut restaurants offer a Bistro Menu. The Three-Cheese Penne Bake contains dairy and egg ingredients and natural flavors of a non-reported source. The Tomato Basil Soup contains several dairy ingredients. The Broccoli Cheddar Soup has chicken broth as its major ingredient. The Garden Side Salad contains cheddar cheese, whey, and Romano cheese powder, all of which can be omitted upon request. All of the other salads on the Bistro Menu contain meat, fish, and/or animal products. The spaghetti dish on the Bistro Kid's Menu contains meat and is made from a beef base.

QDOBA: (About 250 restaurants)
LIST OF MENU ITEMS LABELED AS VEGETARIAN BY QDOBA:
Signature Burritos (with black or pinto beans), Grilled Vegetable Burrito, Vegetarian Burrito, Vegetarian Taco Salad, Vegetarian Taco, Nachos, Tortilla soup

Qdoba said that their protocol is to have designated dishes for all food preparation (cutting boards, utensils, pans, pots, etc.) that are thoroughly cleaned everyday and used for the same purpose the following day. The only pans that do rotate (cleaned thoroughly between uses) are the serving pans (used to bring food out to the serving area from the kitchen). They said that "The grilled vegetables are prepared on the same grill that is used for meat products; however they are never prepared at the same time." Fajita veggies are cooked on the stovetop. The beans are prepared separately from meat products. The rice is prepared separately from meat products. Qdoba restaurants are set up so that patrons build their menu items as they go along a serving area so it is easy to leave off certain components.

Qdoba said that there are no animal-derived ingredients in either the beans or the rice and the tortillas are free of animal ingredients. The fryer oil is used only for frying chips or salad bowls. No meat/egg products are cooked in the same oil. There is a pan release spray used that contains artificial butter flavor, which does not contain animal or dairy components. They said that "the likelihood that our cheese contains animal sourced rennet is highly unlikely. However a few of our suppliers cannot guarantee that our product does not come in contact with trace amounts of animal based rennet." There is no gelatin in either the sour cream or the guacamole. Qdoba indicated that none of their bread products, including chips, contain animal ingredients. (We did not ask specifically about L-cysteine.) Their recipe formulations are considered standard at all Qdoba rest- aurants. They noted that "there can be variations in some items, but this would not interfere with the items considered vegetarian." "There may be differences in suppliers, however all suppliers must meet a standard specification."

SOUPLANTATION/SWEET TOMATOES: (In about 15 states. Concentrated in California, Florida, Arizona, Illinois, Texas) MENU ITEMS CALLED VEGAN BY SOUPLANTATION/SWEET TOMATOES:

Tossed Salads: Fields of Green Citrus Vinaigrette, Mandarin Spinach w/Caramelized Walnuts, Strawberry Fields w/ Caramel- ized Walnuts, Thai Peanut and Red Pepper, Thai Udon and Peanut

Prepared Salads: Aunt Doris' Red Pepper Slaw (Fat-Free), Baja Bean and Cilantro (Low-Fat), Dijon Potato w/Garlic Dill Vinaigrette, Italian White Bean, Lemon Rice w/Cashews, Mandarin Noodles w/ Broccoli (Low-Fat), Mandarin Shells with Almonds (Low-Fat), Roasted Potato w/ Chipotle Chile, Spicy Southwestern Pasta (Low-Fat), Summer Barley w/Black Beans (Low-Fat), Sweet and Sour Broccoli Slaw (Low-Fat), Sweet Marinated Vegetables (Fat-Free), Tabouli, Thai Citrus and Brown Rice, Three Bean Marinade, Tomato Cucumber Marinade

Soups: Classical Minestrone (Low-Fat), India Lentil (Low-Fat), Ratatouille (Fat-Free), Santa Fe Black Bean (Low-Fat), Sweet Tomato Onion (Low-Fat), Vegetarian Harvest

Hot Pastas & Kitchen Favorites: Salsa de Lupe (Fat-Free), Sautéed Balsamic Vegetables

In addition, Souplantation/Sweet Tomatoes lists 83 vegetarian items on their website. Souplantation has a brochure available in its restaurants that lists their most commonly served menu items and gives nutritional information. It contains vegetarian, vegan, or non-vegetarian labels for many items. In that brochure, "vegetarian" and "vegan" are defined. "Vegetarian: Vegetarian items may contain dairy or eggs, but no meat or meat products." "Vegan: Vegan items are made up of all plant-based foods and exclude any animal products."

The brochure states on its last page that "complete ingredient listings are available for viewing upon request." However, Souplantation said the product information pages do not contain complete microingredient information. Above each menu item in the stores, "signs stating 'vegetarian,' 'vegan,' or 'non-vege-tarian'" are posted.

Honey is not in their vegan items. "In general" the rennet used in cheeses is "synthetic" but they can't guarantee it in all cases." Dishes used for replenishing food at the buffet are cleaned between uses but could be used for meat one day and then vegetables the next. Vegan foods are prepared separately from other foods. In general most restaurants are uniform in their standards, but there could be a minimal amount of variation. In emergency situations, the chain would prefer individual restaurants use supplies on hand rather than going to a local supplier.

Souplantation has been around over 30 years. There are 107 stores. They do not define themselves as vegetarian or healthy, but cater to many types of customers. They are able to take a recipe meant for six and convert it to serve thousands.

SUBWAY: Subway is a favorite among many vegetarians because of the choices patrons have in customizing their own subs and salads. As the leading deli-style fast food chain in the United States, Subway continues to offer its Veggie Delite® subs and salads. According to Lanette Kovachi, MS, RD, the Corporate Dietitian at Subway, "Patrons can customize our Veggie Delite® offerings with any bread, vegetable, sauce, and/or cheese that they want."

According to Subway, the Italian Bread, the Hearty Italian Bread, and the Sourdough Bread are free of animal ingredients, although only the Sourdough Bread is free of sugar. Subway's Wheat Bread contains honey and its Pizza Crust contains milk. Kovachi said, "As of March 2007, we will be using a new wrap that does not contain animal-derived ingredients, including L-cysteine." The wrap does contain sodium stearoyl lactylate of a non-reported source.

The Fat Free Sweet Onion Sauce is the only Subway sauce or dressing that does not contain animal ingredients, although it does contain sugar. The Pizza Sauce contains cheese.

Kovachi also told us that, "most likely" the enzymes in their cheeses "are microbial-based, but our manufacturer states that there are some variables in the manufacturing process and cannot 100% guarantee this."

Concerning the dessert items at Subway, Kovachi reports that the natural flavorings for the cookies are "plant derived unless specified as 'butter flavoring.' Then, it is derived from butter." All of the cookies contain both eggs and dairy.

Subway offers a number of fruit-based beverages that are free of animal ingredients, although they do contain sugar.

Subway is a popular restaurant chain in Canada. Subway's Guide to Canadian Product Ingredients is available on its website, along with those of other countries. On the cover of these Guides, Subway states that the food ingredients listed are "currently the most commonly used... [although] formulas may vary from region to region.... Ingredients may vary from this list due to season, changes and formulas, or use of alternate food suppliers."

TACO BELL: Taco Bell offers many food items that are favorites among people who adhere to meatless diets. This year, like in the past, Taco Bell employees have been very helpful in providing us with ingredient information. Taco Bell has also been known to change its ingredient formulations due to consumer request. (Removing the gelatin from its guacamole and lard from its beans are examples.)

Taco Bell is different from many of the other chains we've researched for this article in that its website lists multiple ingredient statements for certain menu items. We've noted the pertinent differences of interest to vegetarians and vegans here. When in doubt, patrons are advised to check with a particular restaurant to know which ingredient formulation is used at that location.

There are several ingredients of concern to vegetarians and vegans in menu items at Taco Bell. Carmine is in the Red Strips and the Lime-Seasoned Red Strips. These items are served on the Fiesta Taco Salad, but this dish may be ordered without them.

The sour cream contains gelatin derived from a bovine source. Sour cream is served with all of the items made Supreme (i.e. Taco Supreme, Soft Taco Supreme, Burrito Supreme, etc.), the Fiesta Taco Salad, the Nachos Bellgrande®, the 7-Layer Burrito, and the Cheesy Potatoes. All of these items may be ordered without the sour cream.

According to Kathleen Ensley of the Quality Assurance Department at Taco Bell, the L-cysteine in the Chalupa Shell, Flat Bread, Pizza Shell, and the Taco Salad Shell is "animal-based." Nacho Chips, Taco Salad Shells, Mexican Pizza Shells, Caramel Apple Empanadas, Cinnamon Twists, Chalupa Shells, Potato Bites, Red Strips, and certain, unnamed promotional items are all fried together. Taco Bell does not fry any of its meat, although in a letter we were told that "all ingredients are handled by employees in common with other ingredients which may not be acceptable to certain types of vegetarian diets."

Ensley was very helpful in answering our questions. She said, "Every menu item at Taco Bell can be customized." Patrons should request omissions of certain components upon ordering. For example, meatless options on the menu at Taco Bell are listed on their 'Food Facts' webpage and include the 1/2 lb. Cheesy Bean & Rice Burrito, the 7-Layer Burrito, and the Cheesy Fiesta Potatoes. The last two contain sour cream, but this can be omitted upon request. The cheese in each item can be omitted as well.

There are some menu items at Taco Bell that are completely free or almost completely free of all animal products, so no component omission is needed. For example, the pinto beans contain no animal ingredients and may be ordered separately. The guacamole is all vegetable, although it contains sugar. The flour tortilla appears to be free of all animal products but does contain sugar. The Nacho Chips, taco shell, Seasoned Rice, and Express Rice also appear to be free of animal ingredients. In fact, 'vegetarian broth' is listed in the ingredient statements for the rice menu items. This is the first time that the writer has seen a meatless stock listed this way in a major fast food chain's ingredients statement and confirms that Taco Bell is a veggie-friendly restaurant chain.

There are no animal enzymes in Taco Bell's flatbread and tortillas. According to Ensley, Taco Bell cheeses, including the Nacho Cheese Sauce, are made with "vegetable-based" chymosin.

The Pizza Sauce at Taco Bell contains natural flavorings of an unspecified source but appears otherwise all-vegetable. The Pizza Shell contains animal-based L-cysteine.

The following sauces and dressings contain eggs and/or dairy: Avocado Ranch Dressing, Creamy Jalapeño Sauce, Creamy Lime Sauce, Nacho Cheese Sauce, Pepperjack Sauce, and Zesty Dressing.

The Fiesta Salsa, the Green Tomatillo Sauce, the Hot Sauce, the Mild Sauce, and the Red Sauce are listed as being free of animal ingredients. The Fire Sauce is, too, but it contains sugar; the other sauces do not. The Citrus Salsa and the Green Chili Sauce contain natural flavorings of unspecified sources and sugar. The Salsa contains natural flavorings of unspecified sources.

For dessert, the Caramel Apple Empanada contains milk products and sugar. The Cinnamon Twists are all-vegetable, although they do contain sugar.

TACO DEL MAR: (270 stores throughout the U.S.)
MENU ITEMS LABELED AS VEGAN BY TACO DEL MAR: Mondo Vegan (tortilla, guacamole, rice, beans, lettuce & salsa), Mondito Vegan (tortilla, guacamole, rice, beans, lettuce & salsa)

MENU ITEMS LABELD AS VEGETARIAN BY TACO DEL MAR: Mondo Veggie, Mondito Veggie, Mondo Veggie Burrito, Mondito Veggie Burrito, Super Nacho, Cheese Quesadilla, Kid's Burrito, Kid's Quesadilla

There is no lard in their beans, which includes black, pinto, and refried. Their guacamole and sour cream have no gelatin. There is no animal rennet in their Jack cheese. Their tortillas do not contain whey. Taco Del Mar steams their long grain rice apart from meat products and it does not contain animal ingredients. Their enchilada sauce no longer contains fish extract, but this may not be noted everywhere.

They usually have one prep table in the back kitchen and train their team members and franchisees to prep 'like' items at one time/sanitize the work surface/prep next item." There are differences in both ingredients and suppliers between the US and Canada. There will be regional menu variations.

WENDY'S: Wendy's offers a Side Salad that comes with iceberg and romaine lettuce, cucumbers, grape tomatoes, and carrots. Cheddar cheese, which may be ordered as an additional salad component, may be made with animal or microbial rennet, according to Kitty Munger, Communications Manager at Wendy's. The Oriental Sesame Dressing and the Italian Vinaigrette Dressing are free of animal ingredients. The Honey Mustard Dressing contains eggs and sugar (but no honey), while the Fat-Free French Dressing contains honey. The Blue Cheese Dressing contains animal-derived natural flavors. All of the other salad dressings at Wendy's contain egg, milk, and/or animal products.

Munger also told us this about the Southwest Taco Salad: "When a customer orders a Southwest Taco Salad, they get a bowl of salad blend lettuce, cheddar cheese, and tomatoes. Separately, they get a serving of chili (with meat and beans), salad dressing, sour cream, and a bag of seasoned tortilla chips." Readers may note that the cheddar cheese may be made with animal or microbial rennet. The sour cream contains gelatin, and the chili is meat-based. The tortilla strips contain milk. The sour cream, chili, and tortilla strips may be omitted when ordering the Southwest Taco Salad.

The Mandarin Chicken Salad is prepared with the chicken, so it cannot be omitted upon ordering. It is possible to order a side of mandarin oranges. They contain added sugar.

Wendy's serves baked potatoes, which are baked in ovens apart from all meat items. They may be ordered plain. The Buttery Best Spread contains milk products. The broccoli topping for the baked potatoes may be ordered separately from the cheese sauce.

The French fries served at **Wendy's appear free** of animal ingredients, although they are **fried in** oil **along** with meat products. Wendy's serves a side of yogurt and granola. The yogurt contains gelatin. The granola cannot be purchased separately.

Summary: Menu Items That Appear to Be Free of Animal, Egg, and Dairy Ingredients at Some Restaurant Chains

Restaurant Chain	Menu Items
Baja Fresh	Side salad without cheese, rice side dish, black beans or pinto beans without cotija cheese, corn tortilla (Corn tortilla with black beans or pinto beans, rice side dish, and side salad)
Burger King	French fries, Minute Maid® Orange Juice, Minute Maid® Apple Juice
Chipotle	Black beans, flour tortilla, guacamole, cilantro-lime rice, sautéed vegetables, crispy corn taco shell (Burrito, taco, or salad made with black beans, flour tortilla or crispy corn taco shell, guacamole, cilantro-lime rice, and sautéed vegetables)
Domino's	Thin Crust Dough, Pizza Sauce,* Garlic Dipping Sauce, Golden Italian Dressing,* Light Italian Dressing* (Thin Crust with pizza sauce and garden salad without the cheese)
McDonald's	English muffin,* Liquid Margarine, Hotcake Syrup,* Apple Dippers, McDonaldland® Cookies, *Minute Maid® Apple Juice Box, orange juice

Papa John's	Original Pizza Dough, Original Pizza Sauce,* Pizza Sauce Dipping Cup,* Garlic Sauce, Cinnamon Apples,* Bumbleberry Filling* (Original Pizza Dough with Original Pizza Sauce)
Pizza Hut	Thin 'N Crispy® Dough, Hand-Tossed Style Dough, Stuffed Crust Dough, XL Full House™ Dough,* Bistro Dough,* 4ForAll® Dough,* Regular Pizza Sauce, Sweet Pizza Sauce, spaghetti, rotelli, and Veggie Medley of the Pasta Bake entrées, French and Italian Dressings, Light Italian Vinaigrette Dressing,* Vinaigrette Dressing,* Light Italian Dressing* (Pizza made with the doughs named above along with regular pizza sauce or sweet pizza sauce; spaghetti [NOT Bistro spaghetti]; salad with one of the above dressings)
Subway	Italian Bread,* Hearty Italian Bread,* Sourdough Bread, Fat Free Onion Sauce*, Fruizle* (Veggie Delite Sub with the just named breads and choice of vegetables, oil, and vinegar; and a Fruizle)
Taco Bell	Pinto beans, guacamole,* flour tortilla,* nacho chips, taco shell, Seasoned Rice, Express Rice, Fiesta Salsa, Green Tomatillo Sauce, Hot Sauce, Mild Sauce, Red Sauce, Fire Sauce,* Cinnamon Twists* (Taco or burrito with pinto beans, mild sauce, and lettuce; guacamole; and Cinnamon Twists)

| Wendy's | Side Salad, Baked Potato, Broccoli Topping for Potato, Oriental Sesame Dressing,* Italian Vinaigrette Dressing,* Mandarin oranges* (Baked potato with broccoli topping and a side salad) |

All information above is provided to us or published by the restaurant chain. *Items with an asterisk contain sugar. (Foods in parentheses are possible meals you can order with these ingredients.)

Finally, these restaurants are worthy of mentioning even though we don't have full information:

BAKERS DRIVE THRU: Bakers Drive Thru in California features a separate vegetarian section on their website and even offers TVP in some of their dishes. However, as of this writing we were unable to receive specific answers to some questions that vegetarians may have.

UNO CHICAGO GRILL: Uno Chicago Grill also has a separate vegetarian section on their website and some options such as a veggie burger (not vegan), roasted vegetables, pizza with spinach, and soups. But there is a little complexity in making sure you order crusts not sprinkled with cheese containing animal rennet. With some clarity, they should be added to this list.

The Vegetarian Resource Group has been providing information on restaurant chains for more than 20 years. Special thanks to Melanie Campbell, Sonja Helman, Charles Stahler, and Jeanne Yacoubou for their help with this edition. Readers should let us know if they hear of any new vegetarian items being offered at restaurant chains. Write to VRG, PO Box 1463, Baltimore, MD 21203. Our e-mail address is vrg@vrg.org, and our website is <www.vrg.org>.

Low-Cost Quick and Easy Vegan Menus Using Convenience Foods

By Reed Mangels, PhD, RD

Many of us would like to spend less time cooking. If you know what to buy and have some quick-to-prepare ideas, you can have "convenience food" on a budget. We've developed menus using a combination of easy-to-fix meals that are quick, inexpensive, and healthful.

The first set of menus was devised to meet the needs of those aged 19-50 years. The menus for women have around 2,200 calories per day, while the men's menus are around 2,500 calories. If you are very active, you will need more calories. You have several choices; you can eat more of the foods already on the menus, or you can add favorite foods to the menus. Conversely, if you are not very active or wish to lose excess weight, you will need fewer calories. In that case, we recommend cutting out some of the "extras" like margarine, chips, desserts, and vegan mayonnaise.

The menus were planned to meet the average person's needs for most nutrients over a week-long period. Although these menus provide generous amounts of iron, women may require additional iron in the form of an iron supplement.

We used specific brand names of foods but have included information on other foods that can be substituted if you don't care for a particular food.

We were curious about how costly these menus would be. The average cost for 1 day's food for a man was a bit over $6 using conventional fruits and vegetables and around $8 using all organic products. The average cost for one day's food for a woman was around $5.50 using conventional fruits and vegetables and almost $7.50 using all organic products. Pricing was done in the winter in New England, so costs may vary depending on the season, your location, and inflation. If you want to reduce food costs even more, you can buy products when they are on sale; see if your supermarket will offer case discounts for items you use often like soymilk. Also, consider buying store brands instead of name brands, use coupons, and choose fruits and vegetables that are in season.

Day 1 for Female, 19-50 years old

Breakfast:
   1/2 cup calcium-fortified orange juice
   1 medium banana
   2 slices whole-wheat toast with 1 Tablespoon nut butter
      (peanut, almond, cashew, etc.)
   1 cup Wheat Chex cereal or any vegan fortified cereal
      providing 20% of the DV for iron or more per cup
   1 cup Soy Dream Enriched soymilk
Lunch:
   1 bowl of Fantastic Foods Big Bowl of Noodles and Hot
      and Sour Soup or any soup/entrée cup providing 250-300
      calories/cup and at least 8% of the DV for iron per serv-
      ing such as Health Valley Pasta Italiano Soup or Health
      Valley Lentil with Couscous Soup
   10 saltines with 1 Tablespoon nut butter (peanut, almond,
      cashew, etc.)
   1 medium orange
   1/2 cup carrot sticks
Dinner:
   1 Morningstar Farms Harvest Burger on a bun or any
      burger providing at least 15% of the DV for iron such as 2
      Whole Foods Vegan Burgers with a large slice of tomato
   1 medium baked potato
Snack:
   1 cup Soy Dream Enriched soymilk
   1 cup kidney beans mixed with 1 Tablespoon salsa
      served with 1 ounce lowfat tortilla chips

Day 2 for Female, 19-50 years old

Breakfast:
- 1 bagel with 2 teaspoons vegan margarine
- 1 medium orange
- 1 cup Cheerios cereal or any vegan fortified cereal providing 20% of the DV for iron or more per cup
- 1 cup Soy Dream Enriched soymilk

Lunch:
- Sandwich of hummus made with 3/4 cup chickpeas and 2 teaspoons tahini on 2 slices of whole-wheat bread with 3 slices of tomato
- 1 medium apple

Dinner:
- 1 cup of cooked pasta with 1/4 cup marinara sauce
- 1/3 cup carrot sticks
- 1 cup cooked broccoli (frozen or fresh)
- 1 whole-wheat roll
- Juice pop made with 1 cup frozen grape juice

Snack:
- 1/2 cup trail mix (mix of nuts, raisins, and sunflower seeds)
- 1 cup Soy Dream Enriched soymilk

Note: In all the menus, Soy Dream Enriched soymilk can be replaced with Silk soymilk or any other calcium-fortified soymilk that provides at least 25% of the Daily Value (DV) for vitamin D and 20% of the DV for vitamin B12 in an 8-ounce serving.

Day 3 for Female, 19-50 years old

Breakfast:
Scrambled tofu made with 1/2 cup tofu, 1/4 cup onions, and 1 teaspoon oil
1 cup calcium-fortified orange juice
2 slices whole-wheat toast with 2 teaspoons vegan margarine
Lunch:
Sandwich made with 1 large pita bread, 1/2 cup shredded lettuce, 1/4 cup chopped tomato, 1/4 cup grated carrot, and 1 Tablespoon Nayonnaise or any spread providing 25-50 calories or can be omitted
Fantastic Foods Country Lentil soup cup or any soup cup providing 200-300 calories and at least 30% of the DV for iron
1 medium banana
1 cup Soy Dream Enriched soymilk
Dinner:
1/2 cup kidney beans with 1 cup cooked quick brown rice and 2 Tablespoons salsa
1 cup frozen mashed squash
1 cup unsweetened applesauce
Snack:
1/2 cup trail mix (mix of nuts, raisins, and sunflower seeds)
1 cup Soy Dream Enriched soymilk

Day 4 for Female, 19-50 years old

Breakfast:
> 1-1/2 cups cooked quick oats with 3 Tablespoons wheat germ, 1/4 cup raisins, and 1 ounce chopped walnuts
>
> 1 cup diced cantaloupe
>
> 1 cup Soy Dream Enriched soymilk

Lunch:
> Burrito made with 1 Garden of Eatin' whole-wheat tortilla or any tortilla providing 125-150 calories and 6% of the DV for iron, 1/2 cup black beans, and 1 Tablespoon salsa
>
> 1 ounce lowfat tortilla chips served with 1/4 cup salsa

Dinner:
> 6 ounces calcium-fortified V-8 juice
>
> Stir-fry made with 1/2 cup diced tofu, 1 cup frozen stir-fry vegetables, 2 Tablespoons soy sauce, 1-1/2 cups cooked quick brown rice, and 1 teaspoon oil
>
> 3 graham crackers

Snack:
> 1 cup Soy Dream Enriched soymilk
>
> 3 cups popped popcorn sprinkled with 1 Tablespoon Vegetarian Support Formula nutritional yeast

Day 5 for Female, 19-50 years old

Breakfast:
    1 English muffin with 1 Tablespoon jelly
    1 cup calcium-fortified orange juice
Lunch:
    Baked tofu made with 4 ounces tofu and 1 Tablespoon
        soy sauce
    1 large sweet potato
    1 Imagine Foods Chocolate Pudding Cup or any product
        providing 120-200 calories such as other flavors of
        Imagine pudding cups, ZenDon soy pudding cup, 2
        Sweet Nothings Bars, 2 Soy Dream Lil' Dreams, 2 Whole
        Foods Frozen Fruit Bars, or 1/2 cup frozen dessert
Dinner:
    1 Yves the Good Dog or any vegan hot dogs providing
        75-90 calories, at least 20% of the DV for iron, and at least
        3% of the DV for zinc such as 2 Yves Tofu Dogs
    1 cup vegetarian baked beans
    1-1/2 cups cooked kale (frozen or fresh)
    2 tomato slices
    1 bagel
    1 baked apple made with 1 medium apple, 1/4 cup
        chopped dates, and 1 Tablespoon granulated sweetener
    1 cup Soy Dream Enriched soymilk
Snack:
    1 ounce walnuts
    1/4 cup raisins
    1 cup Soy Dream Enriched soymilk

Day 6 for Female, 19-50 years old

Breakfast:
- 1 cup Wheat Chex cereal or any vegan fortified cereal providing 20% of the DV for iron or more per cup with 1 medium peach, sliced, and 1 cup Soy Dream Enriched soymilk
- 2 slices whole-wheat toast

Lunch:
- 1 sandwich made with 2 slices whole-wheat bread, 2 Tablespoons nut butter (peanut, almond, cashew, etc.), and 1 Tablespoon jelly
- 1/3 cup carrot sticks
- 1 cup grapes
- 1 cup Soy Dream Enriched soymilk

Dinner:
- 1/2 cup kidney beans with 1 cup cooked pasta and 1/2 cup marinara sauce
- 1 Garden of Eatin' whole-wheat tortilla or any tortilla providing 125-150 calories and 6% of the DV for iron
- 1 medium orange
- 1 cup cooked collard greens (frozen or fresh)

Snack:
- 1 kiwi fruit
- 1/4 cup soynuts
- 10 whole-wheat crackers

Don't forget, although these menus provide generous amounts of iron, women may require additional iron in the form of an iron supplement.

Day 7 for Female, 19-50 years old

Breakfast:
    1-1/2 cups cooked quick oats with 2 Tablespoons wheat germ

    1 English muffin with 2 teaspoons vegan margarine

    1 cup calcium-fortified apple juice

Lunch:
    Sandwich made with 2 slices whole-wheat bread, 2 ounces Yves Veggie Bologna Slices or any deli slice providing 50-100 calories and 20% of the DV for iron in a serving such as Lightlife's Smart Deli Bologna Style (3 slices) or Yves Veggie Salami Slices (4 slices), 1 Tablespoon Nayonnaise or any spread providing 25-50 calories or omitted, 1/3 cup shredded lettuce, and 2 slices tomato

    1 wedge watermelon

    1 cup Soy Dream Enriched soymilk

Dinner:
    1/2 cup chickpeas and 3/4 cup peas with 1 Tablespoon tahini on 1-1/2 cups cooked couscous

    Smoothie made with 1 cup Soy Dream Enriched soymilk, 3 ounces soft tofu, 1 medium frozen banana, 1/2 cup strawberries, and 1 Tablespoon maple syrup

Snack:
    Hummus made with 1/3 cup chickpeas and 1 teaspoon tahini

    1/3 cup carrot sticks

    1/2 cup celery

Day 1 for Male, 19-50 years old

Breakfast:
   1 cup calcium-fortified orange juice
   1 medium banana
   2 slices whole-wheat toast with 1 Tablespoon nut butter
      (peanut, almond, cashew, etc.)
   1 cup Wheat Chex cereal or any vegan ready-to-eat cereal
   1 cup Soy Dream Enriched soymilk
Lunch:
   1 bowl of Fantastic Foods Big Bowl of Noodles and Hot
      and Sour Soup or any soup/entrée cup providing 250-300
      calories/cup such as Fantastic Foods Big Bowl of Italian
      Tomato Noodle, Health Valley Pasta Italiano Soup, or
      Health Valley Lentil with Couscous Soup
   10 saltines with 2 Tablespoons nut butter (peanut, almond,
      cashew, etc.)
   1 medium orange
   1/2 cup carrot sticks
Dinner:
   1 Morningstar Farms Harvest Burger or any vegan burger
      such as Whole Foods 365 Vegan Burger, Lightlife Meat-
      less Lightburgers, Boca Vegan Burger, Gardenburger
      Garden Vegan, or Amy's California Burger on a bun with
      a large slice of tomato
   1 large baked potato
Snack:
   1 cup Soy Dream Enriched soymilk
   1 cup of kidney beans mashed with 1 Tablespoon salsa
   1 ounce lowfat tortilla chips

Day 2 for Male, 19-50 years old

Breakfast:
    1 bagel with 2 teaspoons vegan margarine
    1 medium orange
    1 cup Wheat Chex cereal or any vegan ready-to-eat cereal
    1 cup Soy Dream Enriched soymilk
Lunch:
    2 hummus sandwiches made with 3/4 cup chickpeas and
      2 teaspoons tahini on 4 slices of whole-wheat bread with
      3 slices of tomato
    1 medium apple
Dinner:
    1 cup cooked pasta with 1/4 cup marinara sauce
    1/3 cup carrot sticks
    1 cup cooked broccoli (frozen or fresh)
    2 whole-wheat rolls
    2 teaspoons vegan margarine
    Juice pop made with 1 cup frozen grape juice
Snack:
    1/2 cup trail mix (mix of nuts, raisins, sunflower seeds)
    1 cup Soy Dream Enriched soymilk

Note: In all the menus, Soy Dream Enriched soymilk can be re-placed with Silk soymilk or any other calcium-fortified soymilk that provides at least 25% of the Daily Value (DV) for vitamin D and 20% of the DV for vitamin B12 in an 8-ounce serving.

Day 3 for Male, 19-50 years old

Breakfast:
    1 cup calcium-fortified orange juice
    Scrambled tofu made with 1/2 cup tofu, 1/4 cup onions,
      and 2 teaspoons oil
    2 slices whole-wheat toast with 2 teaspoons vegan
      margarine

Lunch:
    Sandwich made with 1-1/2 large whole-wheat pitas filled
      with 1/2 cup shredded lettuce, 1/4 cup chopped tomato,
      1/4 cup grated carrots, and 1 Tablespoon Nayonnaise or
      any vegan spread providing 25-50 calories or can be
      omitted
    Fantastic Foods Country Lentil soup cup or any soup cup
      providing 200-300 calories such as Fantastic Foods Cha-
      Cha Chili, Black Bean Soup, Split Pea Soup, Couscous
      with Lentils Soup, Five Bean Soup; or Health Valley
      Black Bean Soup or Chili
    1 medium banana
    1 cup Soy Dream Enriched soymilk

Dinner:
    3/4 cup kidney beans with 1 cup quick brown rice and 2
      Tablespoons salsa
    1 Garden of Eatin' whole-wheat tortilla or any tortilla
      providing 125-150 calories per tortilla
    1 cup frozen mashed squash
    1 cup unsweetened applesauce

Snack:
    1/2 cup trail mix (mix of nuts, raisins, sunflower seeds)
    1 cup Soy Dream Enriched soymilk

Day 4 for Male, 19-50 years old

Breakfast:
- 1-1/2 cups quick rolled oats with 2 Tablespoons wheat germ, 1/4 cup chopped dates, and 1 ounce chopped walnuts
- 1 cup diced cantaloupe
- 2 slices whole-wheat toast with 1 Tablespoon nut butter (peanut, almond, cashew, etc.)
- 1 cup Soy Dream Enriched soymilk

Lunch:
- Burrito made with 1 Garden of Eatin' whole-wheat tortilla or any tortilla providing 125-150 calories per tortilla, 1/2 cup black beans, and 1 Tablespoon salsa
- 1 ounce lowfat tortilla chips
- 1/4 cup salsa
- 1 medium apple

Dinner:
- 6 ounces calcium-fortified V-8 juice
- Stir-fry made with 1/2 cup tofu cubes, 1 cup frozen stir-fry vegetable mix, 2 Tablespoons soy sauce, 1 teaspoon oil, and 1-1/2 cups cooked quick brown rice
- 3 graham crackers

Snack:
- 1 cup Soy Dream Enriched soymilk
- 3 cups popped popcorn with 1 Tablespoon Vegetarian Support Formula nutritional yeast

Day 5 for Male, 19-50 years old

Breakfast:
   1 vegan English muffin with 1 Tablespoon jelly
   1 cup grape juice

Lunch:
   Baked tofu made with 4 ounces sliced tofu and 1
      Tablespoon soy sauce
   1 large sweet potato
   1 Imagine Foods Chocolate Pudding Cup or any product
      providing 120-200 calories such as other flavors of
      Imagine pudding cups, ZenDon soy pudding cup, 2
      Sweet Nothings Bars, 2 Soy Dream Lil' Dreams, 2 Whole
      Foods Frozen Fruit Bars, or 1/2 cup frozen dessert

Dinner:
   2 Yves the Good Dogs or any vegan dogs providing 150-
      180 calories and at least 3% of the DV for zinc such as 3
      Yves Veggie Dogs or 2 LightLife Jumbos on buns
   1 cup vegetarian baked beans
   1 cup cooked kale (frozen or fresh)
   2 slices tomato
   1 baked apple made with 1 medium apple, 1/4 cup
      chopped dates, and 1 Tablespoon granulated sweetener
   1 cup Soy Dream Enriched soymilk

Snack:
   1 ounce walnuts
   1/4 cup raisins
   1 bagel
   1 cup Soy Dream Enriched soymilk

Day 6 for Male, 19-50 years old

Breakfast:
>1 cup Wheat Chex cereal or any vegan ready-to-eat cereal with 1 medium peach, sliced, and 1 cup Soy Dream Enriched soymilk
>
>2 slices whole-wheat toast

Lunch:
>1-1/2 sandwiches made with 3 slices whole-wheat bread, 3 Tablespoons nut butter (peanut, almond, cashew, etc.), and 1 Tablespoon jelly
>
>1/3 cup carrot sticks
>
>1 cup grapes
>
>1 cup Soy Dream Enriched soymilk

Dinner:
>1 cup cooked pasta with 1/2 cup kidney beans and 1/2 cup marinara sauce
>
>2 Garden of Eatin' whole-wheat tortillas or any tortillas providing 250-300 calories (for 2 tortillas)
>
>1 medium orange
>
>6 ounces Whole Soy fruited yogurt or any vegan yogurt providing 120-170 calories per serving such as Silk cultured soy fruited yogurt

Snack:
>1 kiwi fruit
>
>1/4 cup soynuts
>
>5 whole-wheat crackers

Day 7 for Male, 19-50 years old

Breakfast:
   1-1/2 cups quick oats with 2 Tablespoons wheat germ
   2 English muffins with 2 teaspoons vegan margarine
   1 cup calcium-fortified apple juice
Lunch:
   Sandwich made with 2 slices whole-wheat bread, 2
      ounces Yves Veggie Bologna Slices or any deli slice
      providing 50-100 calories such as as Lightlife's Smart
      Deli Bologna Style (3 slices), Yves Veggie Salami Slices
      (4 slices), Tofurky Deli Slices (1 ounce), or Vegi-Deli
      Slices (1 ounce), 1 Tablespoon Nayonnaise or any
      vegan spread providing 25-50 calories or can be
      omitted, and 1/2 cup shredded lettuce
   1 wedge watermelon
   1 cup Soy Dream Enriched soymilk
Dinner:
   1/2 cup chickpeas and 3/4 cup peas with 1 Tablespoon
      tahini on 1-1/2 cups couscous
   1 whole-wheat roll
   Smoothie made with 1 cup Soy Dream Enriched soymilk,
      3 ounces soft tofu, 1 medium frozen banana, 1/2 cup
      strawberries, and 1 Tablespoon maple syrup
Snack:
   Hummus made with 1/3 cup chickpeas and 1 teaspoon
      tahini
   1/3 cup carrot sticks
   1 cup celery
   5 whole-wheat crackers

Low-Cost Quick and Easy Vegan Menus for Older People

This second set of menus was devised to meet the needs of men and women age 51 years and older. The menus for men have around 2,300 calories per day while the women's menus are around 1,900 calories. If you are very active, you will need more calories. You have several choices; you can eat more of the foods already on the menus or you can add favorite foods to the menus. Conversely, if you are not very active, you will need fewer calories. In that case, we recommend cutting out some of the "extras" like margarine, chips, desserts, and vegan mayonnaise.

The menus were planned to meet the average person's needs for most nutrients over a week-long period. A vitamin D supplement (5 micrograms for people age 51-70 years old, 10 micrograms for those over age 70) is recommended if your sunlight exposure is limited.

We used specific brand names of foods but have included information on other foods that can be substituted if you don't care for a particular food.

We were curious about how costly these menus would be. The average cost for 1 day's food for a man was a bit over $5.50 using conventional fruits and vegetables and around $7.70 using all organic products. The average cost for one day's food for a woman was around $5.00 using conventional fruits and vegetables and almost $6.40 using all organic products. Pricing was done in the winter in New England so may vary depending on the season, your location, and inflation. If you want to reduce food costs even more, you can buy products when they are on sale, see if your supermarket will offer case discounts for items you use often like soymilk, and choose fruits and vegetables that are in season.

Day 1 for Female, 51+ years old

Breakfast:
- 1/2 cup calcium-fortified orange juice
- 1 medium banana
- 2 slices whole-wheat toast with 1 Tablespoon nut butter (peanut, almond, cashew, etc.)
- 1 cup Wheat Chex cereal or any vegan fortified cereal providing at least 10% of the DV for calcium and 15% of the DV for zinc per cup
- 1 cup Soy Dream Enriched soymilk

Lunch:
- 1 bowl of Fantastic Foods Big Bowl of Noodles and Hot and Sour Soup or any soup/entrée cup providing 250-300 calories/cup, 8 or more grams of protein per cup, and at least 8% of the DV for iron per serving such as Health Valley Lentil with Couscous Soup, Black Bean Chili, Texas-Style Chili, Black Bean with Couscous Soup, Thai Rice, Cantonese Rice, Shiitake Rice, or Pasta Italiano Soup; or Fantastic Foods Jamaican Rice Bowl, Tex-Mex Rice Bowl, Black Bean Salsa Couscous, Country Lentil Soup, Cha-Cha Chili, or 5 Bean Soup
- 10 saltines with 1/2 Tablespoon nut butter (peanut, almond, cashew, etc.)
- 1 medium orange
- 1/2 cup carrot sticks

Dinner:
- 1 Morningstar Farms Harvest Burger or any burger providing at least 140 calories, 18 grams of protein, 8% of the DV for calcium, and 6% of the DV for iron such as 2 Whole Foods Vegan Burgers on a bun with a large slice of tomato
- 1 medium baked potato

Snack:
- 1 cup Soy Dream Enriched soymilk
- 3/4 cup kidney beans mixed with 1 Tablespoon salsa served with 1 ounce lowfat tortilla chips

Day 2 for Female, 51+ years old

Breakfast:
- 1 bagel with 2 teaspoons vegan margarine
- 1 medium orange
- 1 cup Wheat Chex cereal or any vegan fortified cereal providing 10% of the DV for calcium or more per cup
- 1 cup Soy Dream Enriched soymilk

Lunch:
- Hummus sandwich made with 3/4 cup chickpeas and 2 teaspoons tahini on 2 slices of whole-wheat bread with 3 slices of tomato
- 1 medium apple

Dinner:
- 1 cup of cooked pasta with 1/4 cup marinara sauce
- 1/3 cup carrot sticks
- 1 cup cooked broccoli (frozen or fresh)
- 1 whole-wheat roll

Snack:
- 1/4 cup roasted, unsalted soynuts
- 1 cup Soy Dream Enriched soymilk

Note: In all the menus, Soy Dream Enriched soymilk can be replaced with Silk soymilk or any other calcium-fortified soymilk that provides at least 25% of the Daily Value (DV) for vitamin D and 20% of the DV for vitamin B12 in an 8-ounce serving.

Day 3 for Female, 51+ years old

Breakfast:
> Scrambled tofu made with 1/2 cup tofu, 1/4 cup onions, and 1 teaspoon oil
>
> 1/2 cup calcium-fortified orange juice
>
> 2 slices whole-wheat toast

Lunch:
> Sandwich made with 1 large pita bread, 1/2 cup shredded lettuce, 1/4 cup chopped tomato, and 1/4 cup grated carrot
>
> Fantastic Foods Country Lentil soup cup or any soup cup providing 200-300 calories and 16 or more grams of protein such as Health Valley Chili or Fantastic Foods Cha-Cha Chili
>
> 1 medium banana
>
> 1 cup Soy Dream Enriched soymilk

Dinner:
> 1/2 cup kidney beans with 1 cup cooked quick brown rice and 2 Tablespoons salsa
>
> 1 cup frozen mashed squash

Snack:
> 1/2 cup trail mix (mix of nuts, raisins, and sunflower seeds)
>
> 1 cup Soy Dream Enriched soymilk

Day 4 for Female, 51+ years old

Breakfast:
>   1-1/2 cups cooked quick oats with 3 Tablespoons wheat
>   germ, 1/4 cup raisins, and 1 ounce chopped walnuts
>   1 cup Soy Dream Enriched soymilk

Lunch:
>   Burrito made with 1 Garden of Eatin' whole-wheat tortilla
>   or any tortilla providing 125-150 calories, 1/2 cup black
>   beans, and 1 Tablespoon salsa
>   1 cup diced cantaloupe

Dinner:
>   6 ounces calcium-fortified V-8 juice
>   Stir-fry made with 1/2 cup diced tofu, 1 cup frozen stir-fry
>   vegetables, 2 Tablespoons soy sauce, 1-1/2 cups
>   cooked quick brown rice, and 1 teaspoon oil

Snack:
>   1 cup Soy Dream Enriched soymilk
>   3 cups popped popcorn with 1 Tablespoon Vegetarian
>   Support Formula nutritional yeast

Don't forget, although these menus provide generous amounts of iron, women may require additional iron in the form of an iron supplement.

Day 5 for Female, 51+ years old

Breakfast:
- 1 English muffin with 1 Tablespoon jelly
- 1 cup calcium-fortified orange juice

Lunch:
- Baked tofu made with 4 ounces tofu and 1 Tablespoon soy sauce
- 1 large sweet potato

Dinner:
- 2 Yves the Good Dogs or any vegan hot dogs providing 150-175 calories and 26 or more grams of protein such as 3 Yves Veggie Dogs or 2 Lightlife Jumbos
- 1 cup vegetarian baked beans
- 1-1/2 cups cooked kale (frozen or fresh)
- 2 tomato slices
- 1 baked apple made with medium apple, 1/4 cup chopped dates, and 1 Tablespoon granulated sweetener
- 1 cup Soy Dream Enriched soymilk

Snack:
- 1 ounce walnuts
- 1/4 cup raisins
- 1 cup Soy Dream Enriched soymilk

Day 6 for Female, 51+ years old

Breakfast:
    1 cup Wheat Chex cereal or any vegan fortified cereal
    with 1 medium peach, sliced, and 1 cup Soy Dream
    Enriched soymilk
    1 slice whole-wheat toast
Lunch:
    1 sandwich made with 2 slices whole-wheat bread, 2
    Tablespoons nut butter (peanut, almond, cashew, etc.),
    and 1 Tablespoon jelly
    1/3 cup carrot sticks
    1 cup grapes
    1 cup Soy Dream Enriched soymilk
Dinner:
    1/2 cup kidney beans with 1 cup cooked pasta and 1/2 cup
    marinara sauce
    1 Garden of Eatin' whole-wheat tortilla or any tortilla
    providing 125-150 calories
    1 medium orange
    1 cup cooked collard greens (frozen or fresh)
Snack:
    1/4 cup soynuts

Day 7 for Female, 51+ years old

Breakfast:
  1-1/2 cups cooked quick oats with 2 Tablespoons wheat
    germ
  1 English muffin
  1/2 cup calcium-fortified apple juice

Lunch:
  Sandwich made with 2 slices whole-wheat bread, 2
    ounces Yves Veggie Bologna Slices or any deli slice
    providing 50-100 calories and 12 or more grams of
    protein per serving such as as Lightlife's Smart Deli
    Bologna Style (4 slices), Yves Veggie Salami Slices
    (4 slices), or Vegi-Deli Chicken Style slices (1 ounce),
    1/2 cup shredded lettuce, and 2 Slices tomato
  1 wedge watermelon
  1 cup Soy Dream Enriched soymilk

Dinner:
  1/2 cup chickpeas with 1 Tablespoon tahini on 1-1/2 cups
    cooked couscous
  Smoothie made with 1 cup Soy Dream Enriched soymilk,
    3 ounces soft tofu, 1 medium frozen banana, 1/2 cup
    strawberries, and 1 Tablespoon maple syrup

Snack:
  Hummus made with 1/4 cup chickpeas and 1 teaspoon
    tahini
  1/3 cup carrot sticks
  1/2 cup celery

Day 1 for Male, 51+ years old

Breakfast:
- 1 cup calcium-fortified orange juice
- 1 medium banana
- 2 slices whole-wheat toast with 1 Tablespoon nut butter (peanut, almond, cashew, etc.)
- 1 cup Wheat Chex cereal or any vegan ready-to-eat cereal with at least 25% of the DV for zinc per serving
- 1 cup Soy Dream Enriched soymilk

Lunch:
- 1 bowl of Fantastic Foods Big Bowl of Noodles and Hot and Sour Soup or any soup/entrée cup providing 240-300 calories/cup and 8 or more grams of protein per cup such as Health Valley Lentil with Couscous Soup or Fantastic Foods Big Bowl of Noodles Spicy Thai, Country Lentil Soup, Cha-Cha Chili, or 5 Bean Soup
- 10 saltines with 1 Tablespoon nut butter (peanut, almond, cashew, etc.)
- 1 medium orange
- 1/2 cup carrot sticks

Dinner:
- 1 Morningstar Farms Harvest Burger or any veggie burger providing at least 140 calories and 18 grams of protein such as 2 Whole Foods Vegan Burgers on a bun with a large slice of tomato
- 1 medium baked potato

Snack:
- 1 cup Soy Dream Enriched soymilk
- 1 cup of kidney beans mashed with 1 Tablespoon salsa
- 1 ounce lowfat tortilla chips

Day 2 for Male, 51+ years old

Breakfast:
- 1 bagel
- 1 medium orange
- 1 cup Wheat Chex cereal or any vegan ready-to-eat cereal
- 1 cup Soy Dream Enriched soymilk

Lunch:
- 2 hummus sandwiches made with 3/4 cup chickpeas and 2 teaspoons tahini on 4 slices of whole-wheat bread with 3 slices of tomato
- 1 medium apple

Dinner:
- 1 cup cooked pasta with 1/4 cup marinara sauce and 1/2 cup tofu cubes
- 1/3 cup carrot sticks
- 1 cup cooked broccoli (frozen or fresh)
- 2 whole-wheat rolls
- 2 teaspoons vegan margarine

Snack:
- 1/3 cup roasted, unsalted soynuts
- 1 cup Soy Dream Enriched soymilk

Note: In all the menus, Soy Dream Enriched soymilk can be re-placed with Silk soymilk or any other calcium-fortified soymilk that provides at least 25% of the Daily Value (DV) for vitamin D and 20% of the DV for vitamin B12 in an 8-ounce serving.

Day 3 for Male, 51+ years old

<u>Breakfast</u>:
    1 cup calcium-fortified orange juice
    Scrambled tofu made with 1/2 cup tofu, 1/4 cup onions,
       and 2 teaspoons oil
    2 slices whole-wheat toast
<u>Lunch</u>:
    Sandwich made with 1-1/2 large whole-wheat pitas filled
       with 1/2 cup shredded lettuce, 1/4 cup chopped
       tomato, 1/4 cup grated carrots, and 1 Tablespoon
       Nayonnaise or any vegan spread providing 25-50
       calories or can be omitted
    Fantastic Foods Country Lentil soup cup or any soup cup
       providing 200-300 calories and 16 or more grams of
       protein per cup such as Health Valley Chili or Fantastic
       Foods Cha-Cha Chili
    1 medium banana
    1 cup Soy Dream Enriched soymilk
<u>Dinner</u>:
    3/4 cup kidney beans with 1 cup quick brown rice and
       2 Tablespoons salsa
    1 Garden of Eatin' whole-wheat tortilla or any tortilla
       providing 125-150 calories per tortilla
    1 cup frozen mashed squash
    1 cup unsweetened applesauce
<u>Snack</u>:
    1/4 cup roasted, unsalted soynuts
    1 cup Soy Dream Enriched soymilk

Day 4 for Male, 51+ years old

Breakfast:
> 1-1/2 cups quick rolled oats with 2 Tablespoons wheat germ, 1/4 cup chopped dates, and 1 ounce chopped walnuts
>
> 2 slices whole-wheat toast with 1 Tablespoon nut butter (peanut, almond, cashew, etc.)
>
> 1 cup Soy Dream Enriched soymilk

Lunch:
> Burrito made with 1 Garden of Eatin' whole-wheat tortilla or any tortilla providing 125-150 calories per tortilla, 1/2 cup black beans, and 1 Tablespoon salsa
>
> 1 ounce lowfat tortilla chips
>
> 1/4 cup salsa
>
> 1 medium apple

Dinner:
> Stir-fry made with 3/4 cup tofu cubes, 1 cup frozen stir-fry vegetables, 2 Tablespoons soy sauce, 1 teaspoon oil, and 1-1/2 cups cooked quick brown rice
>
> 1 cup diced cantaloupe

Snack:
> 1 cup Soy Dream Enriched soymilk
>
> 3 cups popped popcorn sprinkled with 1 Tablespoon Vegetarian Support Formula nutritional yeast

Day 5 for Male, 51+ years old

<u>Breakfast</u>:
    1 English muffin with 1/2 Tablespoon jelly
    1 cup grape juice
<u>Lunch</u>:
    Baked tofu made with 4 ounces sliced tofu and 1 Table-
        spoon soy sauce
    1 large sweet potato
    1 ounce walnuts
    1/4 cup raisins
<u>Dinner</u>:
    2 Yves the Good Dogs or any vegan hot dogs providing
        150-175 calories and 26 or more grams of protein such
        as 3 Yves Veggie Dogs or 2 Lightlife Jumbos on buns
    1 cup vegetarian baked beans
    1 cup cooked kale (frozen or fresh)
    2 slices tomato
    1 baked apple made with medium apple, 1/4 cup chopped
        dates, and 1 Tablespoon granulated sweetener
    1 cup Soy Dream Enriched soymilk
<u>Snack</u>:
    1 bagel
    1 cup Soy Dream Enriched soymilk

Day 6 for Male, 51+ years old

Breakfast:
- 1 cup Wheat Chex cereal or any vegan ready-to-eat cereal with 1 medium peach, sliced, and 1 cup Soy Dream Enriched soymilk
- 2 slices whole-wheat toast

Lunch:
- 1-1/2 sandwiches made with 3 slices whole-wheat bread, 3 Tablespoons nut butter (peanut, almond, cashew, etc.), and 1 Tablespoon jelly
- 1/3 cup carrot sticks
- 1 cup grapes
- 1 cup Soy Dream Enriched soymilk

Dinner:
- 1 cup cooked pasta with 1/2 cup kidney beans and 1/2 cup marinara sauce
- 1 Garden of Eatin' whole-wheat tortilla or any tortillas providing 125-150 calories per tortilla
- 1 medium orange
- 6 ounces Whole Soy fruited yogurt or any vegan yogurt providing 120-170 calories and 4 or more grams of protein per serving such as White Wave Silk Cultured Soy

Snack:
- 1/4 cup soynuts
- 1/2 cup Soy Dream Enriched soymilk

Day 7 for Male, 51+ years old

Breakfast:
  1-1/2 cups quick oats with 2 Tablespoons wheat germ
  2 English muffins
  1/2 cup calcium-fortified apple juice

Lunch:
  Sandwich made with 2 slices whole-wheat bread, 2 ounces Yves Veggie Bologna Slices or any deli slice providing 50-100 calories and 12 or more grams of protein per serving such as Lightlife's Smart Deli Bologna Style (4 slices), Yves Veggie Salami Slices (4 slices), or Vegi-Deli Chicken Style Slices (1 ounce), 1 Tablespoon Nayonnaise or any vegan spread providing 25-50 calories or can be omitted, and 1/2 cup shredded lettuce
  1 wedge watermelon
  1 cup Soy Dream Enriched soymilk

Dinner:
  1/2 cup chickpeas and 3/4 cup peas with 1 Tablespoon tahini on 1-1/2 cups couscous
  1 whole-wheat roll
  Smoothie made with 1 cup Soy Dream Enriched soymilk, 3 ounces soft tofu, 1 medium frozen banana, 1/2 cup strawberries, and 1 Tablespoon maple syrup

Snack:
  Hummus made with 1/3 cup chickpeas and 1 teaspoon tahini
  1/3 cup carrot sticks
  1 cup celery

RECIPES

The toughest barriers to quick and easy vegetarian cooking are the habits we have developed throughout our lifetime. Once you break that mental resistance, ideas for meals will come to you naturally, meal preparation will become routine and go much faster.

This section has some ideas to get you started. You may want to adjust the amount of spices to your taste. Eliminate salt and soy sauce or tamari and use low sodium tomato sauce and tomato paste if you are on a low sodium diet. If you are on a lowfat diet, when a recipe calls for oil for sautéing vegetables, use slightly more water or vegetable broth instead of the oil.

Recipes were analyzed using Nutritionist IV and manufacturer's information. Optional ingredients were omitted. If ingredient choices were listed (i.e. green or red cabbage), the first ingredient was used in analysis. If a range of servings was specified (i.e. 4-6), the lowest number of servings was used for analysis.

Breakfast Ideas

BROILED GRAPEFRUIT
(Serves 4)

2 large grapefruits, sliced in half, seeds removed
2 Tablespoons maple syrup
1/2 teaspoon cinnamon

Loosen grapefruit sections with a knife. Place grapefruit halves fruit side up on a baking pan and spread 1/2 Tablespoon maple syrup on each half. Sprinkle 1/8 teaspoon cinnamon on each grapefruit half and place under a broiler for 7 minutes. Serve warm.

Total calories per serving: 98
Fat: <1 gram   Total Fat as % of Daily Value: <1%
Protein: 2 grams   Iron: 1 mg   Carbohydrate: 24 grams
Calcium: 81 mg   Dietary fiber: 11 grams

APPLESAUCE
(Serves 6)

6 apples, diced finely
1 Tablespoon cinnamon
1 teaspoon nutmeg
2 oranges, peeled and sliced
Water

Put about 1/3-inch of water in a large pot. Add all the ingredients and cook over medium heat until the apples are soft, stirring occasionally. For variety you can add 1/4 cup raisins.

Total calories per serving: 103
Fat: 2 grams   Total Fat as % of Daily Value: 2%
Protein: 1 gram   Iron: <1 mg   Carbohydrate: 26 grams
Calcium: 27 mg   Dietary fiber: 4 grams

OATMEAL/APPLES/RAISINS AND CINNAMON
(Serves 4)

1 cup rolled oats
3 cups water
2 apples, chopped
1/2 cup raisins
1 teaspoon cinnamon

Heat the above ingredients together in a pot over medium heat for about 5 minutes until oats are cooked. Stir occasionally to prevent sticking.

Total calories per serving: 173
Fat: 2 grams   Total Fat as % of Daily Value: 3%
Protein: 4 grams   Iron: 1 mg   Carbohydrate: 38 grams
Calcium: 24 mg   Dietary fiber: 3 grams

CORNMEAL MUSH
(Serves 2)

1/2 cup quick cooking cornmeal
1-1/2 cups water
1/2 cup chopped fresh fruit (blueberries, bananas, straw-
berries, etc.)

Cook cornmeal in water according to directions on the box, adding chopped fruit just before serving.

Total calories per serving: 163
Fat: 1 gram   Total Fat as % of Daily Value: 2%
Protein: 3 grams   Iron: 2 mg   Carbohydrate: 36 grams
Calcium: 5 mg   Dietary fiber: 3 grams

CINNAMON/SLICED APPLE TOAST
(Serves 6)

6 slices whole wheat bread or English muffins
2-3 apples, thinly sliced
1 Tablespoon brown sugar (optional)
1 Tablespoon vegan margarine
1/2 teaspoon cinnamon

Toast bread. Place several slices of apple, dots of margarine, sprinkle of brown sugar, and a dash of cinnamon on toast or muffin. Place under a broiler until the margarine melts.

Total calories per serving: 114
Fat: 3 grams   Total Fat as % of Daily Value: 5%
Protein: 3 grams   Iron: 1 mg   Carbohydrate: 20 grams
Calcium: 24 mg   Dietary fiber: 1 gram

CORNBREAD AND BLUEBERRIES
(Serves 6)

8-ounce box vegan cornbread mix (Beware: some mixes contain lard!)
1 cup blueberries

Preheat oven to 350 degrees. Add blueberries to batter prepared from a cornbread mix. Pour into lightly oiled 9-inch square cake pan. Bake until done at 350 degrees (approximately 15 minutes).

Total calories per serving: 161
Fat: 4 grams   Total Fat as % of Daily Value: 6%
Protein: 3 grams   Iron: 1 mg   Carbohydrate: 30 grams
Calcium: 1 mg   Dietary fiber: 1 gram

EGGLESS BANANA PANCAKES
(Serves 2)

1/2 cup rolled oats
1/2 cup whole wheat pastry flour or unbleached white flour
1/2 cup cornmeal (white or yellow)
1 Tablespoon baking powder
1-1/2 cups water
2 large ripe bananas, sliced or mashed
2 teaspoons oil

Mix all the ingredients together in a bowl. Use about 1/4 cup of batter per pancake, poured into lightly oiled preheated frying pan. Fry over low heat on one side until light brown, then flip over and fry on the other side until done.

Variations: Add chopped apples, raisins, or blueberries to the batter before frying.

Total calories per serving: 482
Fat: 8 grams   Total Fat as % of Daily Value: 12%
Protein: 12 grams   Iron: 4 mg   Carbohydrate: 97 grams
Calcium: 306 mg   Dietary fiber: 9 grams

EGGLESS FRENCH TOAST
(Serves 3-4)

3 ripe bananas
1 cup soy or rice milk
2 Tablespoons molasses or maple syrup
1/4 teaspoon cinnamon
7 slices whole wheat bread
2 teaspoons oil

Mash bananas in a bowl. Add soy or rice milk, molasses or maple syrup, and cinnamon. Stir well.
   Soak bread in above mixture. Fry in lightly oiled frying pan on both sides over medium heat until lightly brown.

Total calories per serving: 380
Fat: 9 grams   Total Fat as % of Daily Value: 14%
Protein: 10 grams   Iron: 4 mg   Carbohydrate: 70 grams
Calcium: 121 mg   Dietary fiber: 2 grams

HASH BROWN POTATOES
(Serves 4)

2 teaspoons oil
4 large white potatoes, cleaned and thinly sliced
1 large onion, chopped
1/2 teaspoon garlic powder
1/4 teaspoon paprika
Salt and pepper to taste

Heat oil in a frying pan over a medium-high heat. Add potatoes and onion. Add seasonings and stir-fry until potatoes are soft (about 15 minutes).

Total calories per serving: 307
Fat: 3 grams   Total Fat as % of Daily Value: 5%
Protein: 6 grams   Iron: 4 mg   Carbohydrate: 66 grams
Calcium: 31 mg   Dietary fiber: 7 grams

Beverages

HOT APPLE CIDER
(Serves 8)

1/2 gallon apple cider
1 lemon, sliced thinly
1-1/2 teaspoons cinnamon
1/4 teaspoon nutmeg

Heat all the above ingredients in a large pot over medium heat, stirring occasionally, until heated through. Serve warm in mugs.

Total calories per serving: 127
Fat: <1 gram   Total Fat as % of Daily Value: <1%
Protein: <1 grams   Iron: 1 mg   Carbohydrate: 36 grams
Calcium: 23 mg   Dietary fiber: <1 grams

BLENDED FRUIT DRINK
(Serves 4)

3 ripe bananas, sliced
6 strawberries
4 cups chilled orange juice

Blend all the ingredients above in a blender and serve.

Variations: Use different fruit juices and or other fruits such as peaches and apples.

Total calories per serving: 195
Fat: 1 gram   Total Fat as % of Daily Value: 2%
Protein: 3 grams   Iron: 1 mg   Carbohydrate: 48 grams
Calcium: 29 mg   Dietary fiber: 2 grams

QUICK CASHEW MILK
(Serves 4)

1 cup raw cashews
3 cups water

Blend the cashews and water in a blender for 5 minutes and refrigerate. Use as a beverage or in recipes calling for milk. Shake well before serving.

Total calories per serving: 196
Fat: 16 grams   Total Fat as % of Daily Value: 25%
Protein: 5 grams   Iron: 2 mg   Carbohydrate: 11 grams
Calcium: 16 mg   Dietary fiber: 2 grams

EASY ALMOND NUT MILK
(Serves 2)

1/2 cup almonds
1-1/2 cups boiling water

Blend almonds and boiling water in a blender for about 3 minutes at a high speed. Strain through muslin or cheesecloth. (The remaining pulp can be used in burgers or vegetable/nut loaves.) Shake milk well before serving.

Total calories per serving: 172
Fat: 15 grams   Total Fat as % of Daily Value: 24%
Protein: 8 grams   Iron: 2 mg   Carbohydrate: 6 grams
Calcium: 114 mg   Dietary fiber: 3 grams

MILK SHAKE
(Serves 3)

3 cups chilled nut milk (see above recipes)
6 Tablespoons cocoa or carob powder
2/3 cup shredded coconut
Sweetener to taste (maple syrup, etc.)

Blend above ingredients together in a blender at a high speed for 2 minutes. Serve immediately.

Total calories per serving (using cashew milk): 373
Fat: 24 grams   Total Fat as % of Daily Value: 37%
Protein: 8 grams   Iron: 4 mg   Carbohydrate: 35 grams
Calcium: 32 mg   Dietary fiber: 5 grams

SPARKLING SELTZER
(Serves 1)

8 ounces seltzer (salt-free)
2 Tablespoons frozen juice concentrate (orange, grapefruit, lemon, grape, etc.)

Pour chilled seltzer into a glass. Add frozen juice concentrate. Stir well, and enjoy!

Variation: Add ½ cup juice instead of frozen concentrate to ½ cup seltzer.

Total calories per serving (using orange juice concentrate): 56
Fat: <1 grams   Total Fat as % of Daily Value: <1%
Protein: 1 grams   Iron: <1 mg   Carbohydrate: 14 grams
Calcium: 19 mg   Dietary fiber: <1 grams

Salads and Dressings

COLESLAW
(Serves 4)

1/2 medium head green cabbage, shredded
4 carrots, grated
1/2 cup lemon juice
1/2 cup eggless mayonnaise (found in natural foods stores)

Mix all the ingredients together in a large bowl. Chill and toss before serving.

Variations: Add grated apples, crushed pineapple, raisins, and/ or toasted sunflower seeds.

Total calories per serving: 129
Fat: 6 grams   Total Fat as % of Daily Value: 9%
Protein: 2 grams   Iron: 1 mg   Carbohydrate: 16 grams
Calcium: 65 mg   Dietary fiber: 3 grams

A HEFTY SALAD
(Serves 4)

1 stalk celery, diced
1 large carrot, grated
1 clove garlic, minced (optional)
1/2 cup toasted sunflower or pumpkin seeds
2 Tablespoons eggless mayonnaise or dressing of choice
Salt and pepper to taste
1/2 pound lettuce or raw spinach leaves

Mix ingredients (except lettuce or spinach leaves) well in a large bowl and serve on ½ pound lettuce or raw spinach leaves.

Total calories per serving (including lettuce): 139
Fat: 11 grams   Total Fat as % of Daily Value: 17%
Protein: 5 grams   Iron: 2 mg   Carbohydrate: 8 grams
Calcium: 42 mg   Dietary fiber: 3 gram

STUFFED TOMATO SALAD
(Serves 5)

5 large ripe tomatoes
8-ounce can chickpeas (or about 1 cup precooked chick-
**   peas)**
1 stalk celery, chopped (optional)
Salt and pepper to taste

Scoop out tomatoes, saving pulp to use as a sauce. Fill tomatoes with chickpeas and celery.   Season with salt and pepper. Garnish with sauce and lettuce or sprouts.

Total calories per serving: 80
Fat: 2 grams   Total Fat as % of Daily Value: 3%
Protein: 3 grams   Iron: 1 mg   Carbohydrate: 15 grams
Calcium: 24 mg   Dietary fiber: 5 grams

CUCUMBER SALAD
(Serves 6)

3 cucumbers, sliced
1/2 cup white vinegar
1 small onion, minced
Pepper to taste

Mix all the ingredients together in a bowl. Serve immediately; however, the salad tastes better if allowed to sit in the refrigerator for a day or two. Store in a jar.

Total calories per serving: 26
Fat: <1 gram   Total Fat as % of Daily Value: <1%
Protein: 1 grams   Iron: 1 mg   Carbohydrate: 6 grams
Calcium: 25 mg   Dietary fiber: <1 gram

BEET SALAD
(Serves 4)

2 large beets, grated
1/2 medium head cabbage, shredded
3 carrots, grated
Handful of raisins
1 apple, diced
1/4 cup lemon juice
1/4 cup oil
1/4 cup water

Toss all the ingredients together in a large bowl and mix well.

Variations: Use raw sweet potato instead of beets. Add sunflower seeds, crushed pineapple, or other fruit.

Total calories per serving: 232
Fat: 14 grams   Total Fat as % of Daily Value: 21%
Protein: 3 grams   Iron: 1 mg   Carbohydrate: 27 grams
Calcium: 71 mg   Dietary fiber: 4 grams

SUMMER FRUIT SALAD
(Serves 12)

Large fresh pineapple
6 large pieces other fruit (i.e. apples, peaches, plums, etc.)
3 Tablespoons shredded coconut

Stand pineapple upright and cut it in half vertically. Carve out pineapple into bite size pieces. Cut up additional fruit into small pieces. Mix all the fruit together and pour back into pineapple shell. Sprinkle with shredded coconut and serve chilled.

Total calories per serving (using apples, peaches, and plums): 65
Fat: 1 gram   Total Fat as % of Daily Value: 2%
Protein: 1 gram   Iron: <1 mg   Carbohydrate: 15 grams
Calcium: 7 mg   Dietary fiber: 2 grams

POTATO SALAD AND OLIVES
(Serves 4)

4 large white potatoes, peeled and cubed into small pieces
Water
10-ounce box frozen mixed vegetables
1 small onion, chopped finely
1/3 cup black olives, drained and sliced
1 teaspoon celery seed
Salt and pepper to taste
1/2 cup eggless mayonnaise

Cover potatoes with water in a large pot and cook until tender over medium heat. Drain potatoes. At the same time, cook mixed vegetables in a separate pot until tender. Drain vegetables. Mix the ingredients together in a large bowl. Season and add mayonnaise according to your taste.

Variations: Instead of frozen vegetables, add raw vegetables such as finely chopped celery and/or carrots. Add finely chopped parsley. You may also want to use canned pre-cooked Irish potatoes to save more time.

Total calories per serving: 348
Fat: 12 grams   Total Fat as % of Daily Value: 18%
Protein: 9 grams   Iron: 4 mg   Carbohydrate: 55 grams
Calcium: 80 mg   Dietary fiber: 8 grams

MACARONI SALAD
(Serves 6)

3 cups pre-cooked macaroni
2 stalks celery, diced
1 carrot, diced
1 cup peas (frozen or fresh), cooked
1 small onion, finely chopped
Eggless mayonnaise to taste
Salt and pepper to taste

Mix all the ingredients together in a large bowl.

Variations: Add sliced pickles, other vegetables, or olives.

Total calories per serving (using ½ cup mayonnaise): 152
Fat: 4 grams   Total Fat as % of Daily Value: 6%
Protein: 4 grams   Iron: 1 mg   Carbohydrate: 6 grams
Calcium: 9 mg   Dietary fiber: 2 grams

TOMATO SALAD
(Serves 4)

4 tomatoes, cut into 1/2-inch wedges
2 Tablespoons oil
1/4 cup water
1 teaspoon lemon juice
2 cloves garlic, minced
Oregano and salt to taste

Mix all the ingredients together in a bowl and serve.

Total calories per serving: 89
Fat: grams   Total Fat as % of Daily Value: 11%
Protein: 1 gram   Iron: 1 mg   Carbohydrate: 6 grams
Calcium: 9 mg   Dietary fiber: 2 grams

CRANBERRY SALAD
(Serves 12)

12 ounces fresh or frozen cranberries
1/2 cup orange juice or apple juice
1 cup raisins
1 cup shredded coconut
2 stalks celery, chopped finely
1 apple, chopped finely
1/4 cup chopped walnuts (optional)

Blend cranberries, juice, and raisins together in a blender. Pour in to a large bowl and add coconut, celery, apple, and walnuts if desired. Toss well before serving.

Total calories per serving: 102
Fat: 3 grams   Total Fat as % of Daily Value: 5%
Protein: 1 gram   Iron: 1 mg   Carbohydrate: 20 grams
Calcium: 14 mg   Dietary fiber: 2 grams

SWEET RAINBOW DELIGHT
(Serves 6)

3 apples, grated
3 carrots, grated
1/3 cup shredded coconut
1/2 cup raisins

Toss all the ingredients together in a bowl and serve.

Variation: Add chopped dates instead of raisins.

Total calories per serving: 116
Fat: 2 grams   Total Fat as % of Daily Value: 26%
Protein: 1 gram   Iron: 1 mg   Carbohydrate: 26 grams
Calcium: 21 mg   Dietary fiber: 3 grams

RAW VEGETABLE PLATTER
(Serves 12)

Chop up into bite-size pieces 3 to 4 pounds of vegetables including: celery, carrots, broccoli, tomatoes, squash, and mushrooms. Arrange on a large platter. Serve with your favorite dips and spreads or the dressings below.

Nutritional breakdown will vary depending upon vegetables and dressings selected.

SWEET FRENCH DRESSING
(Makes 2 cups)

1 cup oil
2 oranges, peeled and seeds taken out
2 Tablespoons lemon juice
1 Tablespoon white vinegar
1 teaspoon paprika
1 teaspoon salt
Slice of onion, minced

Blend all the ingredients together in a blender for 3 minutes and serve over your favorite salad or raw vegetables.

Total calories per 2 Tablespoon serving: 129
Fat: 14 grams   Total Fat as % of Daily Value: 22%
Protein: <1 gram   Iron: <1 mg   Carbohydrate: 2 grams
Calcium: 7 mg   Dietary fiber: <1 gram

LEMON/APPLE/GARLIC DRESSING
(Makes 3 cups)

1 cup white vinegar
1-1/2 cups water
2 Tablespoons lemon juice
2 cloves garlic, minced
1/4 teaspoon pepper
1/4 teaspoon salt
1 apple — peeled, cored and chopped

Blend all the ingredients together in a blender for 3 minutes.

Total calories per 2 Tablespoon serving: 5
Fat: <1 grams   Total Fat as % of Daily Value: <1%
Protein: <1 gram   Iron: <1 mg   Carbohydrate: 2 grams
Calcium: 2 mg   Dietary fiber: <1 gram

RED BEET DRESSING
(Makes 2 cups)

1 beet, peeled and chopped
1 cup orange juice
1/2 cup oil
1 clove garlic, minced
Salt and pepper to taste

Blend all the ingredients together in a blender for 3 minutes.

Total calories per 2 Tablespoon serving: 69
Fat: 7 grams   Total Fat as % of Daily Value: 11%
Protein: <1 gram   Iron: <1 mg   Carbohydrate: 2 grams
Calcium: 2 mg   Dietary fiber: <1 gram

Soups

VEGETABLE RICE SOUP
(Serves 6-8)

1 cup white rice
6 cups water
1/2 cup parsley, chopped
10-ounce box frozen mixed vegetables
1 medium onion, chopped
Pepper and salt to taste

Cook all the ingredients in a large pot over medium heat until rice is tender (about 30 minutes).

Total calories per serving: 153
Fat: <1 gram   Total Fat as % of Daily Value: <1%
Protein: 4 grams   Iron: 2 mg   Carbohydrate: 34 grams
Calcium: 25 mg   Dietary fiber: 2 grams

FRESH TOMATO SOUP
(Serves 4)

1 large onion, chopped
5 small ripe tomatoes, chopped
1-1/2 cups water
1 teaspoon dried parsley flakes or 2 teaspoons fresh parsley,
    minced
Dash of pepper and salt

Combine ingredients in a large pot. Cook over medium heat for 15 minutes. Cool a few minutes; then blend in a blender, reheat, and serve warm.

Total calories per serving: 36
Fat: <1 gram   Total Fat as % of Daily Value: <1%
Protein: 1 gram   Iron: 1 mg   Carbohydrate: 8 grams
Calcium: 12 mg   Dietary fiber: 2 grams

CREAMED CARROT SOUP
(Serves 6)

1 pound carrots, chopped
1 large onion, chopped
1-1/2 Tablespoons oil
6 cups water
1/2 teaspoon salt
1/3 cup fresh parsley, finely chopped

Sauté the chopped onions and carrots in oil for 5 minutes in a large pot. Add water, salt, and parsley. Bring to a boil. Reduce heat, cover, and simmer for 20 more minutes. Puree mixture in a blender and reheat.

Total calories per serving: 72
Fat: 4 grams   Total Fat as % of Daily Value: 6%
Protein: 1 gram   Iron: 1 mg   Carbohydrate: 10 grams
Calcium: 29 mg   Dietary fiber: 2 grams

CREAM OF BROCCOLI SOUP
(Serves 8)

1 pound broccoli, chopped
1/2 pound mushrooms, chopped
1 small onion, chopped
1 teaspoon tarragon
3 cups soy and/or rice milk
Salt and pepper to taste

Steam vegetables and onion together for 10 minutes. Blend half of the steamed vegetables in a blender or food processor along with 1-1/2 cups soy and/or rice milk. Pour into a large pot. Blend remaining steamed vegetables and soy and/or rice milk. Add to pot. Season with tarragon, salt, and pepper, and reheat for 5 minutes over medium heat. Add water if you prefer thinner soup. Serve warm.

Total calories per serving: 86
Fat: 3 grams   Total Fat as % of Daily Value: 5%
Protein: 6 grams   Iron: 1 mg   Carbohydrate: 10 grams
Calcium: 60 mg   Dietary fiber: 3 grams

CREAMED ZUCCHINI/POTATO SOUP
(Serves 6)

1 small onion, chopped
3 Tablespoons oil
3 or 4 medium zucchini, chopped
2 large white potatoes, scrubbed and cut into small cubes
6 cups water
1/2 cup rolled oats
1/2 teaspoon salt
2 Tablespoons fresh parsley, finely chopped

Sauté onion in oil in a large pot for 2 minutes. Add chopped zucchini and cubed potatoes. Sauté for 5 minutes longer. Add water, oats, and seasoning. Simmer for 15 minutes. Puree mixture in a blender, reheat, and serve warm.

Total calories per serving: 168
Fat: 8 grams   Total Fat as % of Daily Value: 12%
Protein: 4 grams   Iron: 2 mg   Carbohydrate: 23 grams
Calcium: 35 mg   Dietary fiber: 3 grams

Lunch Ideas

MOCK "TUNA" SALAD
(Serves 3)

1 cup chickpeas (canned or pre-cooked and drained)
1 stalk celery
1/2 small onion, finely chopped
3 Tablespoons eggless mayonnaise
Salt and pepper to taste

Mash the chickpeas in a small bowl. Add remaining ingredients and mix well. Spread on whole grain bread as a sandwich or serve on a bed of lettuce.

Total calories per serving: 122
Fat: 5 grams   Total Fat as % of Daily Value: 8%
Protein: 4 grams   Iron: 1 mg   Carbohydrate: 17 grams
Calcium: 35 mg   Dietary fiber: 5 grams

SPINACH/MUSHROOM SANDWICH
(Serves 6)

10-ounce box frozen spinach
1 cup mushrooms, sliced finely
1 pint sour cream (look for non-dairy sour cream found in
**   natural food stores and kosher supermarkets)**
6 thick slices whole grain bread or English muffins

Cook spinach per instruction on box and drain well. Place cooked spinach and sliced mushrooms on the bread. Cover with sour cream. Place in toaster oven under low heat until hot. Serve warm.

Total calories per serving: 184
Fat: 9 grams   Total Fat as % of Daily Value: 14%
Protein: 7 grams   Iron: 2 mg   Carbohydrate: 22 grams
Calcium: 354 mg   Dietary fiber: 4 grams

QUICK PIZZA
(Serves 6)

3 English muffins or 6 slices whole wheat bread
1 cup tomato sauce
6 slices vegan cheese
Italian seasoning to taste
1/2 cup chopped vegetables (i.e. sliced onion, chopped
green peppers, sliced mushrooms, and/or sliced olives)

Toast the English muffin or bread. Spoon sauce over top of bread. Lay slices of cheese on top. Season to taste. Put on optional toppings and place pizza in a toaster oven until the cheese melts (approximately 5-10 minutes). Serve warm.

Total calories per serving: 128
Fat: 3 grams   Total Fat as % of Daily Value: 5%
Protein: 4 grams   Iron: 1 mg   Carbohydrate: 20 grams
Calcium: 244 mg   Dietary fiber: 1 gram

POTATO PANCAKES
(Serves 6)

3 cups cooked white potatoes, mashed
1 small onion, chopped
Salt and pepper to taste
1/4 cup fresh parsley, finely chopped (optional)
2 Tablespoons oil

Mix the mashed potatoes, onion, and seasonings together. Heat oil in a large frying pan. Pour pancakes onto heated pan and fry on each side until light brown (about 8 minutes per side). Serve warm alone or with applesauce.

Total calories per serving: 113
Fat: 5 grams   Total Fat as % of Daily Value: 8%
Protein: 2 grams   Iron: <1 mg   Carbohydrate: 17 grams
Calcium: 6 mg   Dietary fiber: 1 gram

CORN FRITTERS
(Serves 6)

2 cups corn kernels (fresh, frozen, or canned and drained)
1 cup flour
1-1/2 Tablespoons corn starch
1-1/4 cups water
1 Tablespoon oil

Mix all the ingredients (except oil) in a medium-size bowl. Pour batter into a lightly oiled frying pan over medium heat and fry for 3-5 minutes. Turn fritters over and continue frying for 3 minutes longer. Serve warm.

Variations: Instead of corn use other chopped vegetables.

Total calories per serving: 157
Fat: 3 grams   Total Fat as % of Daily Value: 5%
Protein: 4 grams   Iron: 1 mg   Carbohydrate: 18 grams
Calcium: 3 mg   Dietary fiber: 2 grams

COUSCOUS/SQUASH BURGERS
(Makes 12 — serve 2 burgers per person)

3 cups cooked couscous (about ¾ of 10-ounce box)
1-1/2 pounds grated zucchini and/or yellow squash
1/2 small onion, finely chopped
1/2 cup unbleached white flour
2-1/2 teaspoons marjoram
Salt and pepper to taste
1 Tablespoon oil

Mix all the ingredients (except oil) together. Using wet hands, form 12 flat burgers. Fry for 10 minutes on each side in a lightly oiled frying pan over medium-high heat. Serve warm alone or on whole wheat buns for sandwiches.

Total calories per serving: 176
Fat: 3 grams   Total Fat as % of Daily Value: 5%
Protein: 6 grams   Iron: 1 mg   Carbohydrate: 33 grams
Calcium: 27 mg   Dietary fiber: 6 grams

RICE BURGERS
(Makes 6 burgers)

2 cups rice, cooked (leftover cooked rice is great)
1/2 cup bread crumbs
1 cup mixed vegetables (i.e. celery, carrots, squash,
    broccoli), finely chopped
Salt and pepper to taste
1/3 cup oil

Mix rice, bread crumbs, vegetables, and seasonings together. Using wet hands, form 6 flat burgers. Fry for 8-10 minutes on each side in a lightly oiled frying pan over medium-high heat. Serve warm alone or on whole wheat buns with lettuce for sandwiches.

Variations: Instead of cooked rice, use cooked barley. Also, add a small onion, finely chopped.

Total calories per burger (using celery, carrots, squash, and broccoli): 223
Fat: 13 grams   Total Fat as % of Daily Value: 20%
Protein: 3 grams   Iron: 1 mg   Carbohydrate: 25 grams
Calcium: 18 mg   Dietary fiber: 1 gram

LENTIL BURGERS
(Makes 6)

1 cup lentils, pre-cooked in 2-1/2 cups water and drained
1 small onion, finely chopped
1/2 cup wheat germ
1/2 teaspoon garlic powder
Salt and pepper to taste
1 Tablespoon oil

Mix all the ingredients together. Using wet hands, form 6 patties. Fry for 10 minutes on each side in a lightly oiled frying pan over medium heat. Serve warm alone or on a roll with lettuce and tomato.

Total calories per burger: 147
Fat: 4 grams   Total Fat as % of Daily Value: 6%
Protein: 10 grams   Iron: 3 mg   Carbohydrate: 21 grams
Calcium: 21 mg   Dietary fiber: 4 grams

Side Dishes

CAULIFLOWER AU GRATIN
(Serves 4)

10-ounce box frozen cauliflower
1-1/2 cups bread crumbs
2 teaspoons oil
4 slices vegan cheese, cut into strips
Salt and pepper to taste

Cook cauliflower according to directions on the box and drain. Preheat oven to 350 degrees. Roll cooked cauliflower in bread crumbs and place in oiled baking dish. Add strips of cheese and seasoning. Bake at 350 degrees until cheese melts.

Total calories per serving: 225
Fat: 7 grams   Total Fat as % of Daily Value: 11%
Protein: 8 grams   Iron: 2 mg   Carbohydrate: 34 grams
Calcium: 245 mg   Dietary fiber: 3 grams

SCALLOPED CORN AND TOMATOES
(Serves 6)

2 Teaspoons oil
4 large tomatoes, sliced thickly
15-ounce can corn kernels, drained or 10-ounce box frozen
    corn kernels
1 cup bread crumbs
2 Tablespoons margarine

Preheat oven to 350 degrees. Spread oil in an approximately 8-inch x 2-inch tall round baking dish. Place tomatoes on the bottom and mix in the corn. Top with bread crumbs and dot with margarine. Bake at 350 degrees about 20 minutes or until crumbs are toasted. Serve warm.

Total calories per serving: 201
Fat: 7 grams   Total Fat as % of Daily Value: 11%
Protein: 6 grams   Iron: 1 mg   Carbohydrate: 18 grams
Calcium: 27 mg   Dietary fiber: 4 grams

LEFTOVER POTATO DISH
(Serves 6)

2 Tablespoons oil
2 cups leftover baked or boiled potatoes, sliced
1 large onion, chopped
1 cup leftover cooked vegetables
Paprika, garlic powder, salt, and pepper to taste

Heat oil in a large frying pan over medium-high heat.   Fry
potatoes and onions for 5 minutes.   Add vegetables and
seasonings and continue heating for 5 more minutes.   Serve
warm.

Total calories per serving (using broccoli and carrots): 114
Fat: 5 grams   Total Fat as % of Daily Value: 8%
Protein: 2 grams   Iron: 1 mg   Carbohydrate: 17 grams
Calcium: 21 mg   Dietary fiber: 2 grams

GREEN BEANS WITH HERB SAUCE
(Serves 4)

10-ounce box frozen French-style green beans
1/2 small onion, finely chopped
2 Tablespoons vegan margarine
1 Tablespoon fresh parsley, finely chopped
1/4 teaspoon thyme
1-1/2 Tablespoons lemon juice
Paprika, salt, and pepper to taste

Cook green beans per directions on box and drain. Place cooked green beans in a serving dish. Sauté onion in margarine in a medium-size frying pan over medium heat for 3 minutes. Add remaining ingredients and mix well. Once heated pour over cooked green beans and serve.

Total calories per serving: 72
Fat: 6 grams   Total Fat as % of Daily Value: 9%
Protein: 1 gram   Iron: 1 mg   Carbohydrate: 6 grams
Calcium: 38 mg   Dietary fiber: 1 gram

SAUTÉED MUSHROOMS
(Serves 4)

2 Tablespoons vegan margarine or oil
1 pound mushrooms, cleaned and chopped
1 large onion, finely chopped
Garlic powder, salt, and pepper to taste

Heat margarine or oil in a large frying pan over medium-high heat. Sauté mushrooms and onion for 5 minutes. Season to taste and cook over low heat for 3 minutes longer or until mushrooms are tender. Serve warm.

Total calories per serving: 89
Fat: 6 grams   Total Fat as % of Daily Value: 9%
Protein: 3 grams   Iron: 1 mg   Carbohydrate: 8 grams
Calcium: 14 mg   Dietary fiber: 2 grams

CABBAGE DISH
(Serves 6)

1 Tablespoon oil
1 medium-size head green cabbage, shredded
1/2 cup toasted sesame seeds
6 slices vegan cheese

Sauté cabbage and sesame seeds in oil in a large frying pan over medium-high heat until cabbage is tender. Add strips of cheese and cook over low heat until cheese melts. Serve warm.

Variation: Use lettuce, spinach, or bok choy instead of cabbage.

Total calories per serving: 162
Fat: 10 grams   Total Fat as % of Daily Value: 15%
Protein: 5 grams   Iron: 2 mg   Carbohydrate: 13 grams
Calcium: 362 mg   Dietary fiber: 4 grams

SPANISH RICE
(Serves 3)

1 medium onion, finely chopped
1 large green pepper — cored, seeds removed, and chopped
2 teaspoons oil
1/4 cup water or vegetable broth
1-1/2 cups rice, pre-cooked (leftovers are good)
3 large ripe tomatoes, cubed
8-ounce can tomato sauce
Pepper, cumin, and chili powder to taste

Sauté onion and green pepper in oil in a large frying pan over medium heat for 3 minutes. Add remaining ingredients and cook 10 more minutes, stirring occasionally to prevent sticking. Serve.

Total calories per serving: 222
Fat: 4 grams   Total Fat as % of Daily Value: 6%
Protein: 5 grams   Iron: 3 mg   Carbohydrate: 43 grams
Calcium: 29 mg   Dietary fiber: 4 grams

STUFFED MUSHROOMS
(Serves 4)

12 large mushrooms
1/2 cup vegetable broth or water
1 small ripe avocado
1 small ripe tomato, finely chopped
Pinch of cayenne pepper and garlic powder
Salt to taste

Remove stems from mushrooms. Sauté mushroom caps in broth or water for a few minutes until soft. Remove from heat and allow to cool. Mash avocado in a small bowl. Add tomato and seasonings. Mix well. Stuff mushrooms with avocado mixture and serve.

Total calories per serving: 90
Fat: 7 grams   Total Fat as % of Daily Value: 11%
Protein: 4 grams   Iron: 1 mg   Carbohydrate: 7 grams
Calcium: 8 mg   Dietary fiber: 1 gram

FRIED ZUCCHINI AND SAUCE
(Serves 4)

1 Tablespoon oil
2 pounds zucchini, sliced lengthwise ½-inch thick
Italian seasoning, salt, and pepper to taste
8-ounce can tomato sauce

Fry zucchini slices in oil in a large covered frying pan with seasonings for 5 minutes over medium heat. Flip zucchini over, cover with tomato sauce, and continue cooking over low heat for 10 minutes. Serve warm.

Total calories per serving: 78
Fat: 4 grams   Total Fat as % of Daily Value: 6%
Protein: 3 grams   Iron: 2 mg   Carbohydrate: 16 grams
Calcium: 41 mg   Dietary fiber: 3 grams

SWEET AND SOUR CABBAGE
(Serves 6)

1 small head cabbage (red and/or green), shredded
1 large onion, chopped
2 Tablespoons oil
1/2 cup raisins
1 large apple, grated
1/2 cup water
2 Tablespoons unbleached white flour
2 Tablespoons vinegar
1 Tablespoon brown sugar or other granulated sweetener
2 teaspoons salt
1/2 cup water

Sauté onions and cabbage in oil in a large frying pan over a medium heat for 8 minutes. Add raisins, apple, and 1/2 cup water. Cook 5 minutes longer. In a small jar, shake up flour, vinegar, sugar, salt, and 1/2 cup water. Add to frying pan and cook another 8 minutes. Serve warm.

Variation: Use crushed pineapple instead of grated apple.

Total calories per serving: 142
Fat: 5 grams   Total Fat as % of Daily Value: 8%
Protein: 2 grams   Iron: 1 mg   Carbohydrate: 25 grams
Calcium: 57 mg   Dietary fiber: 3 grams

PASTA DISH
(Serves 4)

3 Tablespoons vegan margarine
1/4 teaspoon each oregano, basil, salt, and black pepper
1/2 teaspoon garlic powder
1/4 cup fresh parsley, finely chopped (optional)
1 pound pasta, cooked and drained
3 Tablespoons vegan Parmesan cheese or nutritional yeast

Melt margarine in a large pot and add seasonings. Stir in cooked pasta, sprinkle on cheese or yeast and serve warm.

Total calories per serving: 509
Fat: 10 grams   Total Fat as % of Daily Value: 15%
Protein: 17 grams   Iron: 4 mg   Carbohydrate: 86 grams
Calcium: 69 mg   Dietary fiber: 0 grams

Main Dishes

RIGATONI COMBINATION
(Serves 6)

1/3 pound rigatoni shells, macaroni, or other pasta
1 large onion, chopped
1 clove garlic, minced
1/2 large green pepper, chopped
2 teaspoons olive oil
8-ounce can tomato sauce
16-ounce can kidney beans, drained
1 teaspoons soy sauce or tamari
1/2 teaspoon chili powder
Pepper and salt to taste

Cook pasta according to package directions. Sauté onion, garlic, and green pepper in oil for 5 minutes in a large pot. Stir in tomato sauce, kidney beans, soy sauce or tamari, and seasonings. Simmer several minutes to heat through. Drain pasta when done cooking and stir into sauce. Serve as is or add hot sauce if desired.

Total calories per serving: 181
Fat: 2 grams   Total Fat as % of Daily Value: 3%
Protein: 8 grams   Iron: 3 mg   Carbohydrate: 33 grams
Calcium: 36 mg   Dietary fiber: 6 grams

TOMATO/EGGPLANT BAKE
(Serves 4)

1 Tablespoon oil
1 small eggplant, peeled and cut into small pieces
15-ounce can stewed tomatoes
1 onion, finely chopped
1 large green pepper, finely chopped

Preheat oven to 350 degrees. Place eggplant, stewed tomatoes, onion, and green pepper in a large oiled baking dish. Bake at 350 degrees until done (approximately 20 minutes). Serve warm.

Total calories per serving: 100
Fat: 4 grams   Total Fat as % of Daily Value: 6%
Protein: 2 grams   Iron: 1 mg   Carbohydrate: 16 grams
Calcium: 54 mg   Dietary fiber: 3 grams

BROCCOLI/KASHA BAKE
(Serves 6)

10-ounce box frozen broccoli
1-1/2 cups kasha, uncooked
4 slices vegan cheese
1 Tablespoon oil

Preheat oven to 350 degrees. Cook broccoli per package directions and drain. Cook kasha in water until done. Mash broccoli and mix well with kasha. Place in a medium-size oiled baking dish. Lay slices of cheese on top. Bake at 350 degrees until cheese melts. Serve warm.

Total calories per serving: 205
Fat: 5 grams   Total Fat as % of Daily Value: 8%
Protein: 7 grams   Iron: 1 mg   Carbohydrate: 36 grams
Calcium: 156 mg   Dietary fiber: 5 grams

VEGETARIAN STEW
(Serves 4)

1/2 cup corn kernels (fresh, frozen, or canned)
1/2 cup lima beans (fresh, frozen, or canned)
1/2 cup potatoes (pre-cooked or canned)
1/2 cup stewed tomatoes
1 medium onion, chopped
1 teaspoon oregano
1/4 cup fresh parsley, finely chopped
Salt and pepper to taste

Mix above ingredients in a large pot. Cook over low heat until heated through (about 12 minutes). Serve alone or over rice.

Total calories per serving: 87
Fat: <1 gram   Total Fat as % of Daily Value: <1%
Protein: 3 grams   Iron: 1 mg   Carbohydrate: 15 grams
Calcium: 28 mg   Dietary fiber: 3 grams

LEFTOVER STEW
(Serves 4)

1 Tablespoon oil
1 small onion, chopped
1 green pepper, chopped
3 stalks celery, chopped
1 cup crushed tomatoes
2 cups leftovers (pre-cooked beans, seeds or nuts, raisins, grains, vegetables, olives, etc.)
Salt, pepper, and Italian seasoning to taste

Sauté onion, green pepper, and celery in oil in a large pot. Add tomatoes, leftovers, and seasonings. Cook over medium heat 10-15 minutes and serve warm.

Total calories per serving (using kidney beans and rice): 171
Fat: 4 grams   Total Fat as % of Daily Value: 6%
Protein: 6 grams   Iron: 2 mg   Carbohydrate: 29 grams
Calcium: 52 mg   Dietary fiber: 5 grams

MACARONI/CABBAGE DISH
(Serves 4)

1-1/2 cups macaroni
6 cups water
1/2 medium cabbage, shredded
1 medium onion, chopped
1 large green pepper, chopped
1/2 cup vegetable broth
Salt and pepper to taste

Cook macaroni in boiling water until tender and drain. Meanwhile, sauté cabbage, onion, and green pepper in vegetable broth in a large pot over medium heat for 10 minutes.   Add cooked macaroni and seasoning and heat 5 minutes longer. Serve warm.

Total calories per serving: 187
Fat: 1 gram   Total Fat as % of Daily Value: 2%
Protein: 7 grams   Iron: 2 mg   Carbohydrate: 39 grams
Calcium: 59 mg   Dietary fiber: 3 grams

VEGETABLE POT PIE
(Serves 8)

Crust: This is a quick crust that can be used in many different recipes. (In a rush use a store-bought pie crust.)

2 cups whole wheat pastry flour or unbleached white flour
1/2 teaspoon salt
1/2 cup vegan margarine
1/2 cup water

Mix flour and salt in bowl. Work in margarine with fingers. Add water, stirring as little as possible to form a ball. Divide into 2 equal balls and roll out to 1/8-inch thickness. Prick pie shells and bake in pie pans at 400 degrees for 10 minutes.

Vegetable Filling:

1/2 cup vegetable broth
1 cup onions, chopped
1 cup celery, chopped
1/2 cup carrots, chopped
1-1/4 cups peas (fresh or frozen)

Sauté above ingredients in broth until onions are soft. In a separate bowl mix the following:

1/4 cup oil
1/2 cup unbleached white flour
1-2/3 cups water
1/2 teaspoon garlic powder
1 teaspoon salt
1/3 teaspoon pepper

Preheat oven to 350 degrees. Add above mixture to sautéed vegetables. Pour into one pie shell and cover with the other pie shell. Bake at 350 degrees until crust is brown (approximately 15-20 minutes).

Total calories per serving: 320
Fat: 18 grams   Total Fat as % of Daily Value: 28%
Protein: 7 grams   Iron: 2 mg   Carbohydrate: 34 grams
Calcium: 33 mg   Dietary fiber: 6 grams

VEGETARIAN CHILI
(Serves 6)

1 Tablespoon oil
1 large onion, chopped
3 cloves garlic, minced
1 large green pepper, chopped
3 cups water
1 cup kidney beans (pre-cooked or canned)
4 large ripe tomatoes, chopped
1 cup corn kernels (fresh, frozen, or canned)
1 teaspoon salt
1 teaspoon chili powder
Pepper to taste

In a large pot sauté the onion, garlic, and green pepper in oil over medium heat until the onion is soft. Add water, kidney beans, tomatoes, corn, salt, chili powder, and pepper. Cook 25 minutes longer.

Variations: Add hot peppers, other vegetables such as carrots and celery, or add 2/3 cup bulgur (cracked wheat). Pinto beans may be used instead of kidney beans.

Total calories per serving: 118
Fat: 3 grams   Total Fat as % of Daily Value: 5%
Protein: 5 grams   Iron: 1 mg   Carbohydrate: 15 grams
Calcium: 28 mg   Dietary fiber: 5 grams

RATATOUILLE
(Serves 4)

1/2 cup vegetable broth
3 large ripe tomatoes, chopped
1 large zucchini, chopped
1 small eggplant, cubed
1 large green pepper, chopped
1 large onion, chopped
2-3 cloves garlic, minced

In a large frying pan sauté the tomatoes, zucchini, eggplant, peppers, onions, and garlic in broth over low heat for 15 minutes. Serve warm over a bed of rice or slice of bread.

Total calories per serving: 81
Fat: 1 gram   Total Fat as % of Daily Value: 2%
Protein: 3 grams   Iron: 1 mg   Carbohydrate: 18 grams
Calcium: 36 mg   Dietary fiber: 3 grams

SPAGHETTI AND VEGETABLE SAUCE
(Serves 4)

Cook 1 pound of spaghetti and drain.

Sauce:

2 teaspoons oil
1 large onion, chopped
2 cloves garlic, minced
15-ounce can tomato sauce
6-ounce can tomato paste
1 small zucchini, sliced
2 carrots, chopped
1 cup mushrooms, sliced
Italian seasoning, salt, and pepper to taste

Sauté onion and garlic in oil in a large pot over low heat for 5 minutes. Add sauce, paste, vegetables, and seasoning. Cook 20 minutes longer. Serve warm over cooked pasta.

Total calories per serving: 529
Fat: 5 grams   Total Fat as % of Daily Value: 8%
Protein: 18 grams   Iron: 8 mg   Carbohydrate: 104 grams
Calcium: 65 mg   Dietary fiber: 7 grams

FRIED EGGPLANT
(Serves 4)

1 large eggplant
1/4 cup oil
1 cup bread crumbs (or crushed corn flakes or matzo meal)
1 medium onion, chopped
3 cloves garlic, minced

Slice eggplant. Add one Tablespoon oil to bread crumbs. Dip eggplant slices into crumbs. Fry eggplant, onion, and garlic in remaining oil over medium heat for 10 minutes.

Variations: Top with vegan parmesan cheese, tomato sauce, and/or Italian seasoning.

Total calories per serving: 269
Fat: 15 grams   Total Fat as % of Daily Value: 23%
Protein: 5 grams   Iron: 1 mg   Carbohydrate: 30 grams
Calcium: 50 mg   Dietary fiber: 1 gram

LENTIL STEW
(Serves 6)

1 cup lentils
1 cup macaroni or other pasta
15-ounce can tomato sauce
6-ounce can tomato paste
1 large onion, chopped
1 teaspoon Italian seasoning
1 teaspoon garlic powder
4 cups water

Cook all ingredients in a large pot over medium heat until tender (approximately 20 minutes). Serve warm.

Total calories per serving: 203
Fat: 1 gram   Total Fat as % of Daily Value: 2%
Protein: 11 grams   Iron: 5 mg   Carbohydrate: 39 grams
Calcium: 40 mg   Dietary fiber: 7 grams

ZUCCHINI BAKE
(Serves 4)

2 large zucchini, sliced
4 slices vegan cheese
15-ounce can tomato sauce
Salt and pepper to taste

Preheat oven to 325 degrees. Place alternating layers of zucchini, cheese, and tomato sauce in a medium-size baking dish. Season to taste. Bake at 325 degrees for 20-25 minutes. Serve hot.

Total calories per serving: 95
Fat: 3 grams   Total Fat as % of Daily Value: 5%
Protein: 4 grams   Iron: 2 mg   Carbohydrate: 14 grams
Calcium: 222 mg   Dietary fiber:3 grams

Soy Dishes

Although tofu and tempeh may not be familiar products to you, we have chosen to include them because they are convenient soy food products. Tofu can be found in most supermarkets today. If you've eaten in Chinese restaurants, you probably have eaten some tofu. It would have been called soybean curd. Tofu can be used to make dips and soups, desserts such as strawberry tofu cheesecake, and side or main dishes such as curried tofu or fried tofu, which has a texture similar to fried chicken. Unfortunately, tempeh is still only found in some supermarkets and is more likely to be found in a natural foods store. It is a fermented soy product and has a meaty texture. Tempeh can be prepared in a variety of ways.

TOFU MAYONNAISE DIP
(Serves 8)

16-ounces tofu, drained (soft or silken tofu is best)
1/2 teaspoon prepared mustard
2 teaspoons lemon juice
1 Tablespoon olive or vegetable oil
3 Tablespoons water
1 large clove garlic, minced
1/4 teaspoon salt
1 Tablespoon soy sauce or tamari
1/2 teaspoon Louisiana-style hot sauce (optional)
1/2 teaspoon rice or maple syrup (optional)

Blend all the ingredients in a food processor until very smooth. Use as a dressing for potato, macaroni, or rice salads; or use as a dip for raw vegetables. If you want a simple mayonnaise, omit the last four ingredients.

Total calories per serving: 48
Fat: 3 grams   Total Fat as % of Daily Value: 5%
Protein: 3 grams   Iron: 1 mg   Carbohydrate: 2 grams
Calcium: 17 mg   Dietary fiber: <1 gram

TOFU SPINACH DIP
(Serves 8)

1 large onion, finely chopped
2 cloves garlic, minced
2 Tablespoons oil
1/2 pound tofu, drained (soft or silken tofu is best)
3 Tablespoons mustard or eggless mayonnaise
10-ounce box frozen spinach, pre-cooked
Dash of pepper
Soy sauce or tamari to taste

Sauté onion and garlic in oil in a large frying pan over medium heat for 5 minutes. Pour into a blender cup and add remaining ingredients. Blend until creamy. Chill and serve with crackers and/or raw vegetables.

Total calories per serving: 67
Fat: 5 grams   Total Fat as % of Daily Value: 8%
Protein: 3 grams   Iron: 1 mg   Carbohydrate: 5 grams
Calcium: 69 mg   Dietary fiber: 1 gram

TOFU EGGLESS SALAD
(Serves 6)

1 pound tofu, drained and crumbled (firm tofu is best)
1 stalk celery, finely chopped
1 large carrot, grated
3 Tablespoons sweet pickle relish
2 Tablespoons eggless mayonnaise
Salt, pepper, and dill weed to taste

In a medium-size bowl mix all the ingredients together. Serve on a bed of lettuce or on whole grain toast with lettuce and sprouts.

Total calories per serving: 117
Fat: 6 grams   Total Fat as % of Daily Value: 9%
Protein: 9 grams   Iron: 1 mg   Carbohydrate: 6 grams
Calcium: 139 mg   Dietary fiber: 1 gram

SUMMER TOFU SALAD
(Serves 4)

1/2 pound romaine lettuce leaves, rinsed
1 pound tofu, drained and cut in finger-size pieces (soft or silken tofu is best)
1 stalk celery, chopped
2 scallions, chopped
1 large white radish, chopped
1/4 cup fresh parsley, finely chopped
1 large ripe tomato, chopped
1 Tablespoon soy sauce or tamari
1 teaspoon oil
Salt and pepper to taste

Lay lettuce leaves on 4 small plates. Arrange pieces of tofu around perimeter of each plate leaving an empty circle in the middle. Sprinkle with celery, scallions, radish, and parsley. Put tomato in center of each plate. Drizzle soy sauce or tamari and oil over the entire dish. Season and serve.

Hint: This salad tastes better if it sits a while before serving.

Total calories per serving: 98
Fat: 5 grams   Total Fat as % of Daily Value: 8%
Protein: 7 grams   Iron: 2 mg   Carbohydrate: 8 grams
Calcium: 69 mg   Dietary fiber: 2 grams

SPINACH PIE
(Serves 8)

10-ounce box frozen spinach
1-1/2 cups onion, chopped
3 cloves garlic, minced
2 Tablespoons oil
3 cups crumbled tofu (soft or silken tofu is best)
1 Tablespoon lemon juice
Salt and pepper to taste
1 pre-made pie crust

Cook spinach according to package directions. Sauté onion and garlic in oil in a large pot over medium heat for 3 minutes. Add spinach, tofu, lemon juice, and seasoning. Preheat oven to 350 degrees. Meanwhile, continue cooking spinach/tofu mixture for 5 minutes. Mix well. Pour into pie crust. Bake at 350 degrees for 15-20 minutes until crust is brown.

Total calories per serving: 180
Fat: 11 grams   Total Fat as % of Daily Value: 18%
Protein: 7 grams   Iron: 2 mg   Carbohydrate: 15 grams
Calcium: 87 mg   Dietary fiber: 1 gram

TOFU BURGERS
(Serves 4)

2 cups tofu, crumbled (firm tofu is best)
2 teaspoons garlic powder
1 cup wheat germ
2 teaspoons onion powder
2 Tablespoons soy sauce or tamari
1 teaspoon pepper
1/2 cup fresh parsley, finely chopped
1/2 cup celery, finely chopped
1 Tablespoon oil
1/2 cup water or vegetable broth
2 teaspoons oil for frying

Blend or mash tofu well and add remaining ingredients (except 2 teaspoons oil for frying). (The easiest way to do this is in a food processor, but you can do it by hand.) Mix well. Form patties and fry in a lightly oiled frying pan on both sides until brown (approximately 10 minutes). Serve warm on whole grain bread with lettuce and sliced tomato. Cold leftover burgers are also good.

Variation: Bake burgers instead of frying by first rolling patties in wheat germ. Lay in baking pan and bake at 350 degrees until warm and light brown.

Total calories per serving: 318
Fat: 16 grams   Total Fat as % of Daily Value: 25%
Protein: 24 grams   Iron: 5 mg   Carbohydrate: 19 grams
Calcium: 256 mg   Dietary fiber: <1 gram

FRIED TOFU
(Serves 4)

1 pound tofu, drained and sliced
1/4 cup soy sauce or tamari
1 cup unbleached white flour
2 Tablespoons oil
Salt and pepper to taste

Dip tofu in soy sauce or tamari, then in flour. Season well with salt and pepper, then fry in oil over medium heat in a large frying pan until brown on both sides (approximately 10-15 minutes). Serve warm as is or as a sandwich on whole grain bread with lettuce and tomato.

Variations: Instead of unbleached white flour, use wheat germ or nutritional yeast.

Total calories per serving: 271
Fat: 13 grams   Total Fat as % of Daily Value: 20%
Protein: 14 grams   Iron: 8 mg   Carbohydrate: 27 grams
Calcium: 127 mg   Dietary fiber: 1 gram

CURRIED TOFU WITH PEANUTS
(Serves 4)

1 large onion, finely chopped
2 cloves garlic, minced
3 Tablespoons oil
1/4 cup roasted peanuts, whole or chopped
1 pound tofu, drained and cut into 1-inch cubes
1 teaspoon salt
1 teaspoon curry powder
1-1/2 cups peas (fresh, frozen, or canned)
1 large carrot, chopped

Sauté onion and garlic in oil in large frying pan over medium heat for 3 minutes. Add remaining ingredients and cook for 15 minutes longer. Add a little water if necessary to prevent sticking. Serve warm over a bed of rice.

Variations: Use garlic powder or minced ginger instead of garlic. Also, use different nuts and vegetables.

Total calories per serving: 299
Fat: 20 grams   Total Fat as % of Daily Value: 30%
Protein: 15 grams   Iron: 7 mg   Carbohydrate: 18 grams
Calcium: 156 mg   Dietary fiber: 4 grams

FRIED TEMPEH SANDWICHES
(Serves 4)

8-ounce package tempeh (any variety), sliced into strips
2 Tablespoons oil
1 medium onion, chopped
Salt and pepper to taste
8 slices whole grain bread

Fry tempeh in oil with onions and seasoning over medium heat in a large frying pan until brown on both sides (approximately 10 minutes).   Place tempeh and onions on whole grain bread with sliced tomato, cucumber, mayonnaise or mustard, sprouts, and lettuce.

Total calories per serving (not including tomato, etc.): 322
Fat: 14 grams   Total Fat as % of Daily Value: 22%
Protein: 16 grams   Iron: 3 mg   Carbohydrate: 38 grams
Calcium: 98 mg   Dietary fiber: <1 gram

SPAGHETTI AND TEMPEH SAUCE
(Serves 4)

1 pound spaghetti, pre-cooked and drained

Sauce:

8-ounce package tempeh (any variety), chopped into 1-inch cubes
1/2 teaspoon oregano
Garlic powder and salt to taste
1 small onion, finely chopped (optional)
2 Tablespoons oil
8-ounce can tomato sauce

Sauté tempeh in oil with seasoning and chopped onion if desired in a large frying pan over medium heat for 5 minutes.   Add tomato sauce and heat 5 minutes longer.   Serve warm over cooked spaghetti.

Total calories per serving: 408
Fat: 13 grams   Total Fat as % of Daily Value: 20%
Protein: 26 grams   Iron: 6 mg   Carbohydrate: 98 grams
Calcium: 80 mg   Dietary fiber: 1 gram

Chinese Cuisine

CHINESE MIXED VEGETABLES AND TOFU
(Serves 5)

2 Tablespoons oil
1/2 cup vegetable broth
2 cups vegetables, chopped (i.e. celery, carrots, green
    pepper, bok choy, corn, snow peas)
8 ounces tofu, drained and cubed (firm tofu is best)
Soy sauce or tamari to taste

Stir-fry ingredients in oil and broth in a large frying pan over medium heat for 15 minutes. Serve alone or over a bed of rice.

Total calories per serving (celery, carrots, green pepper, and bok choy): 115
Fat: 8 grams   Total Fat as % of Daily Value: 12%
Protein: 6 grams   Iron: 1 mg   Carbohydrate: 5 grams
Calcium: 93 mg   Dietary fiber: 1 gram

STIR-FRIED VEGETABLES, GINGER, AND RICE
(Serves 6)

1 Tablespoon oil
1/3 cup vegetable broth
3 cups mixed vegetables, chopped
1-1/2 cups pre-cooked rice (leftovers are good)
2 Tablespoons soy sauce or tamari
1/4 teaspoon fresh ginger, grated

Sauté vegetables in oil and broth in a large pot over medium heat for 10 minutes. Add rice, soy sauce or tamari, and ginger to vegetables. Cook 8 minutes longer and serve warm.

Total calories per serving (using broccoli, carrots, and cabbage): 96
Fat: 3 grams   Total Fat as % of Daily Value: 5%
Protein: 3 grams   Iron: 1 mg   Carbohydrate: 16 grams
Calcium: 25 mg   Dietary fiber: 2 grams

VEGETABLE CHOW MEIN
(Serves 6)

2 Tablespoons oil
1/2 cup vegetable broth
3 cups pre-cooked rice (leftovers are good)
1 cup bean sprouts (fresh or canned)
1 stalk celery, chopped
1 large green pepper, chopped
1 large carrot, chopped
2 large ripe tomatoes, chopped
Soy sauce or tamari to taste

Sauté the rice and vegetables with soy sauce or tamari in oil and broth in a large frying pan over medium heat for 15 minutes. Serve warm.

Total calories per serving: 176
Fat: 6 grams   Total Fat as % of Daily Value: 9%
Protein: 3 grams   Iron: 1 mg   Carbohydrate: 29 grams
Calcium: 23 mg   Dietary fiber: 3 grams

MOCK FOO YOUNG
(Serves 2)

10 ounces tofu, crumbled (firm tofu is best)
1/4 cup cornmeal
1 large carrot, grated
Salt and pepper to taste
1/4 teaspoon oregano
1 Tablespoon sesame seeds (optional)
2 teaspoons oil for frying

Blend all the ingredients (except oil for frying) together in a blender. Form four patties and fry on both sides until light brown in a lightly oiled frying pan over medium heat.

Variation: For a totally different taste, cover patties with tomato sauce and sprinkle with vegan cheese.

Total calories per serving: 288
Fat: 13 grams   Total Fat as % of Daily Value: 20%
Protein: 18 grams   Iron: 3 mg   Carbohydrate: 16 grams
Calcium: 260 mg   Dietary fiber: 2 grams

FRIED RICE WITH PEANUTS OR ALMONDS
(Serves 6)

1 large onion, chopped
1 Tablespoon oil
2 cups pre-cooked rice (leftovers are good)
1 large green pepper, chopped
1 stalk celery, chopped
1 cup mushrooms, sliced
1 small zucchini, chopped
2 Tablespoons soy sauce or tamari
1 cup roasted peanuts or almonds, chopped or whole

Sauté onion in oil in a large frying pan over a medium heat for 3 minutes. Add the remaining ingredients and stir-fry 15 minutes.

Total calories per serving: 256
Fat: 15 grams   Total Fat as % of Daily Value: 23%
Protein: 9 grams   Iron: 1 mg   Carbohydrate: 25 grams
Calcium: 42 mg   Dietary fiber: 4 grams

Mexican Fiesta

MEXICAN SUCCOTASH
(Serves 6)

2 Tablespoons oil
1 small onion, chopped
1 pound zucchini, sliced
1 large green pepper, chopped
1/4 cup pimientos, diced
2 large ripe tomatoes, chopped
1-1/2 cups corn kernels (frozen, fresh, or canned)
Salt and pepper to taste

Sauté onion in oil in a large frying pan over medium heat for 3 minutes. Add remaining ingredients and simmer until vegetables are tender (about 10 minutes). Add a little water if necessary to prevent sticking. Serve as a side dish or over a bed of rice.

Total calories per serving: 112
Fat: 5 grams   Total Fat as % of Daily Value: 8%
Protein: 3 grams   Iron: 1 mg   Carbohydrate: 8 grams
Calcium: 18 mg   Dietary fiber: 3 grams

REFRIED BEANS
(Serves 8)

1 large onion, chopped
3 Tablespoons oil
Two 15-ounce cans pinto or kidney beans, drained
6-ounce can tomato paste
3 Tablespoons chili powder

Sauté onion in oil in a large frying pan over a medium heat for three minutes. Add the remaining ingredients and stir-fry for 15 minutes. Serve over tortilla chips or in taco shells with shredded lettuce, chopped tomatoes, hot sauce, olives, etc.

Total calories per serving: 162
Fat: 6 grams   Total Fat as % of Daily Value: 9%
Protein: 6 grams   Iron: 3 mg   Carbohydrate: 22 grams
Calcium: 57 mg   Dietary fiber: 2 grams

EASY TOSTADAS
(Serves 6-8)

Two 1-pound cans vegetarian chili
1 box vegan enchilada shells or flat taco shells
1 cup shredded lettuce
1 large cucumber, peeled and chopped
1 large onion, chopped
1/2 cup shredded vegan cheese (optional)
Taco sauce to taste

Heat chili in a large pot until warm. Preheat oven to 400 degrees. Lay shells in a single layer on a cookie sheet. Spread chili on each shell. Heat at 400 degrees for 5 minutes. Remove from oven and let each person garnish shells with remaining ingredients as desired. Note: This dish tastes good chilled as well. Simply open can and put chili on shells and garnish. This is a terrific dish when traveling.

Total calories per serving: 278
Fat: 2 grams   Total Fat as % of Daily Value: 3%
Protein: 15 grams   Iron: 4 mg   Carbohydrate: 51 grams
Calcium: 103 mg   Dietary fiber: 13 grams

GUACAMOLE
(Serves 4)

1 large or 2 small ripe avocados, peeled and pit(s) removed
1 small ripe tomato, finely chopped
1/4 teaspoon garlic powder
Pinch of cayenne pepper
Salt to taste

Mash avocado in a bowl. Add chopped tomato and seasonings. Mix well and serve on tacos, with chips or crackers, or as a dip with raw vegetables.

Total calories per serving: 100
Fat: 9 grams   Total Fat as % of Daily Value: 14%
Protein: 1 gram   Iron: 1 mg   Carbohydrate: 5 grams
Calcium: 7 mg   Dietary fiber: 2 grams

Spreads and Dips

Spreads can be used for parties, snacks, or light dinners. They not only taste good, but can be nutritious. But like many foods, if you eat too much, the calories will add up. Serve these spreads and dips with lowfat crackers, breads, or raw vegetables such as carrots, celery, peppers, cauliflower, or zucchini.

LENTIL PATE
(Serves 8)

1 cup lentils
2 cups water
1 large onion, finely chopped
4 cloves garlic, minced
1 Tablespoon vegan margarine
1 teaspoon black pepper
1/2 teaspoon vinegar
Water if necessary

Cook lentils in water in a medium-size pot until done. At the same time, sauté onions and garlic in margarine in a separate pot over medium heat for 3 minutes. Add pepper. Mix lentils, onions, garlic, and pepper together. Blend the mixture in a food processor adding water if necessary until well mixed. Add vinegar last. Chill before serving.

Total calories per serving: 85
Fat: 2 grams   Total Fat as % of Daily Value: 3%
Protein: 5 grams   Iron: 2 mg   Carbohydrate: 13 grams
Calcium: 17 mg   Dietary fiber: 3 grams

MUSHROOM/EGGPLANT SPREAD
(Makes about 4 cups)

1 pound eggplant, peeled and chopped into 1-inch cubes
12 ounces portabello mushrooms, finely chopped
Medium onion, finely chopped
2 Tablespoons oil
1/2 teaspoon coriander
1/2 teaspoon cumin
Salt and pepper to taste

Sauté ingredients in a large frying pan over medium-high heat for 10-12 minutes. Mash with a potato masher until a chunky, yet spreadable consistency. Chill and spread on crackers or bread.

Total calories per ¼ cup serving: 30
Fat: 2 grams   Total Fat as % of Daily Value: 3%
Protein: 1 gram   Iron: <1 mg   Carbohydrate: 3 grams
Calcium: 4 mg   Dietary fiber: <1 gram

GARBANZO PEANUT SPREAD
(Serves 8)

16-ounce can chickpeas, drained
3 Tablespoons peanut butter
1/3 cup lemon juice
3/4 cup water or as needed
1 Tablespoon oil
1/8 teaspoon cumin
1/2 teaspoon garlic powder
Salt and pepper to taste

Blend all the ingredients together in a food processor until smooth. Add more water if necessary.

Variation: Instead of using peanut butter, use tahini (sesame butter) and add some sautéed onions and parsley.

Total calories per serving: 125
Fat: 6 grams   Total Fat as % of Daily Value: 9%
Protein: 5 grams   Iron: 1 mg   Carbohydrate: 14 grams
Calcium: 27 mg   Dietary fiber: 5 grams

SPLIT PEA SPREAD

(Serves 6)

1 cup split peas
3-1/4 cups water
1 large carrot, finely chopped
2 stalks celery, finely chopped
1 small onion, finely chopped
1 teaspoon celery seed
Salt and pepper to taste

Bring split peas to a rapid boil in a medium-size pot. Add carrot and celery. Then add onions and seasoning. Cover pot and boil 15 minutes longer. Remove from heat and blend until smooth in a food processor.   Place in a bowl and chill before serving.

Total calories per serving: 125
Fat: <1 gram   Total Fat as % of Daily Value: <1%
Protein: 8 grams   Iron: 2 mg   Carbohydrate: 23 grams
Calcium: 30 mg   Dietary fiber: 2 grams

CHOPPED "LIVER" SPREAD

(Serves 6)

1 Tablespoon oil
1/4 cup water
1/2 pound mushrooms, chopped
1 small onion, chopped
1 cup chopped walnuts
Salt and pepper to taste

Sauté mushrooms and onion in oil and water in a large frying pan over medium heat for 8 minutes. Pour into a food processor. Add walnuts and seasoning. Blend until smooth, adding more water if necessary. Chill before serving.

Total calories per serving: 115
Fat: 10 grams   Total Fat as % of Daily Value: 17%
Protein: 4 grams   Iron: 1 mg   Carbohydrate: 4 grams
Calcium: 12 mg   Dietary fiber: 1 gram

WHITE BEAN SPREAD
(Makes about 2 cups)

19-ounce can white beans, drained
1 stalk celery, finely chopped
Juice of 1/2 small lemon
1/4 teaspoon dill weed
Pepper to taste

Mash white beans in a bowl. Add remaining ingredients and mix well. Chill before serving.

Total calories per ¼ cup serving: 78
Fat: <1 gram   Total Fat as % of Daily Value: <1%
Protein: 5 grams   Iron: 1 mg   Carbohydrate: 14 grams
Calcium: 34 mg   Dietary fiber: 3 grams

AVOCADO/CUCUMBER SPREAD
(Serves 8)

1 small ripe avocado, pit removed
1 large cucumber, peeled and chopped
1/4 teaspoon garlic powder
1/4 teaspoon salt
1/4 teaspoon cayenne

Place all the ingredients in a food processor and blend until creamy. This spread can also be used as a salad dressing.

Total calories per serving: 35
Fat: 3 grams   Total Fat as % of Daily Value: 5%
Protein: 1 gram   Iron: <1 mg   Carbohydrate: 2 grams
Calcium: 8 mg   Dietary fiber: 1 gram

NUT "CHEESE"
(Serves 6)

1/2 cup raw cashews
1/2 cup water
1/4 cup lemon juice
3 Tablespoons oil
1/2 small tomato, finely chopped
Garlic powder and paprika to taste

Blend cashews, water, and lemon juice together in a food processor. Slowly add oil. Then add remaining ingredients and blend well. Chill before serving.

Total calories per serving: 130
Fat: 12 grams   Total Fat as % of Daily Value: 18%
Protein: 2 grams   Iron: 1 mg   Carbohydrate: 5 grams
Calcium: 7 mg   Dietary fiber: 1 gram

Desserts

SPICY DATE NUT SPREAD
(Serves 4)

1/4 pound dates, pitted
1/2 cup hot water
1/2 cup walnuts, chopped
1 large apple, cored and finely chopped
1/4 teaspoon cinnamon
Pinch of ginger powder (optional)

Soak dates in hot water for a few minutes. Put date/water mixture in a food processor. Add remaining ingredients and blend until smooth. Serve on slices of fresh fruit including apples, peaches, and pears.

Total calories per serving: 169
Fat: 6 grams   Total Fat as % of Daily Value: 9%
Protein: 3 grams   Iron: 1 mg   Carbohydrate: 30 grams
Calcium: 19 mg   Dietary fiber: 4 grams

COCONUT CLUSTERS
(Serves 8)

2 cups shredded coconut
4 ripe medium bananas, mashed
1/4 cup cocoa powder or carob powder
1 cup walnuts, chopped (optional)

Preheat oven to 350 degrees. Blend ingredients together in a medium-size bowl. Form clusters on a lightly oiled cookie sheet. Bake for 20 minutes at 350 degrees. Cool, then remove from cookie sheet.

Variation: Instead of cocoa or carob powder, use 1/2 cup chopped fresh fruit such as strawberries.

Total calories per serving: 174
Fat: 9 grams   Total Fat as % of Daily Value: 14%
Protein: 2 grams   Iron: 2 mg   Carbohydrate: 26 grams
Calcium: 11 mg   Dietary fiber: 2 grams

OATMEAL COOKIES
(Makes 40 cookies)

1/2 cup vegan margarine
1-1/2 cups (15 ounces) applesauce
1/2 cup molasses or maple syrup
2 large ripe bananas, peeled
1-3/4 cups whole wheat pastry flour
1 teaspoon baking soda
1 teaspoon baking powder
1 teaspoon cinnamon
1 teaspoon nutmeg
3 cups rolled oats
1/2 cup raisins or chopped dates

Preheat oven to 400 degrees. Cream together margarine, applesauce, molasses or maple syrup, and bananas in a large bowl. Add remaining ingredients and mix well. Drop a rounded Tablespoon of batter at a time on a lightly oiled cookie sheet. Bake 8 minutes at 400 degrees. Allow cookies to cool before removing from cookie sheet.

Variation: Add chopped walnuts or chopped apples to batter.

Total calories per cookie: 84
Fat: 3 grams   Total Fat as % of Daily Value: 5%
Protein: 2 grams   Iron: 1 mg   Carbohydrate: 15 grams
Calcium: 24 mg   Dietary fiber: 1 gram

FRESH FRUIT SALAD AND PEANUT CREME
(Serves 8)

Prepare a fruit salad for 8 people using your favorite fruits in season. If you are in a rush, use canned fruit salad.

Peanut Creme:

1 cup water
2 apples
1 cup peanuts

Blend apples in 1/2 cup water in a food processor. Slowly add peanuts and remaining water as needed until a smooth consistency is reached. Serve over fruit salad.

Total calories per serving (without fruit): 125
Fat: 9 grams   Total Fat as % of Daily Value: 14%
Protein: 5 grams   Iron: <1 mg   Carbohydrate: 9 grams
Calcium: 18 mg   Dietary fiber: 2 grams

Variations: Serve peanut creme over baked apples and pears. You can also experiment with different types of nuts.

RICE PUDDING
(Serves 6)

1 cup rice
2/3 cups raisins
2 large ripe bananas, peeled and mashed
1/2 cup water
1 teaspoon cinnamon
1/4 teaspoon nutmeg

Cook rice with raisins following package instructions in a large pot until done. Preheat oven to 350 degrees. Pour cooked rice and raisins into a food processor. Add the remaining ingredients and blend together for 1 minute. Pour into a medium-size baking dish. Bake for 20 minutes at 350 degrees. Serve warm or chilled.

Total calories per serving: 209
Fat: <1 gram   Total Fat as % of Daily Value: <1%
Protein: 3 grams   Iron: 2 mg   Carbohydrate: 50 grams
Calcium: 14 mg   Dietary fiber: 2 grams

TOFU PIE AND QUICK CRUST
(Serves 8)

Pie crust:

2 cups lowfat granola
1/4 cup vegan margarine

Preheat oven to 350 degrees. Blend granola and margarine
together in a medium-size bowl. Press into 8-inch pie pan and
bake for 10 minutes at 350 degrees. Leave oven on while you
prepare pie filling below.

Pie filling:

4 dates
1 pound tofu, drained (soft or silken tofu is best)
3 Tablespoons chocolate syrup
2 Tablespoons oil

Soak dates in a little boiling water for 5 minutes and drain. Place
pie filling ingredients in a blender cup and blend until creamy,
adding a little water if necessary.

Pour filling into pie crust and bake for 20 minutes at 350
degrees. Chill in the refrigerator before serving.

Variation: Instead of chocolate syrup use fresh chopped fruit
such as strawberries, peaches, or blueberries.

Total calories per serving: 231
Fat: 12 grams   Total Fat as % of Daily Value: 18%
Protein: 6 grams   Iron: 2 mg   Carbohydrate: 28 grams
Calcium: 30 mg   Dietary fiber: 2 grams

Seasonal Party Ideas for Twelve People

SUMMERTIME MENU:

Fruit Salad (recipe below)

2 dozen bagels and/or rolls with vegan cream cheese (such as *Tofutti* brand) or vegan margarine

Raw vegetable Platter (recipe below)

Guacamole (see page 151) or Avacado/Cucumber Spread (see page 156)

2 pounds assortment of nuts and seeds

2 pounds variety of dried fruit

2 gallons fruit juices and/or Blended Fruit Drink (see page 104)

1-1/2 dozen ears hot steamed corn (can be done indoors or outdoors over a barbecue)

FRUIT SALAD
(Serves 12)

1/2 ripe watermelon, cut lengthwise
10 peaches, pits removed and quartered
1 pint strawberries, sliced
1 pint blueberries
1 cup raisins
1 cup shredded coconut (optional)

Scoop out bite-size pieces of watermelon and place in a large bowl. Add remaining ingredients. Mix well and pour back into hollowed out watermelon shell. Keep chilled until serving.

Total calories per serving: 126
Fat: 1 gram   Total Fat as % of Daily Value: 2%
Protein: 2 grams   Iron: 1 mg   Carbohydrate: 31 grams
Calcium: 24 mg   Dietary fiber: 4 grams

RAW VEGETABLE PLATTER
(Serves 12)

5 large ripe tomatoes, sliced
1 pound carrots, sliced lengthwise into sticks
3 cucumbers, peeled and sliced
4 stalks celery, sliced lengthwise into sticks
1 pound olives, drained
1 pound chopped broccoli or cauliflower
1 pound zucchini, sliced lengthwise into sticks

Arrange all the vegetables on a large platter.

Total calories per serving: 120
Fat: 9 grams   Total Fat as % of Daily Value: 14%
Protein: 4 grams   Iron: 2 mg   Carbohydrate: 14 grams
Calcium: 91 mg   Dietary fiber: 5 grams

AUTUMN MENU:

Creamed Carrot Soup (see page 116 and double the recipe)
Ratatouille (see page 136 and double the recipe)
4 cups rice precooked
Curried Tofu with Peanuts (see page 144 and triple the recipe)
1 dozen fresh apples (assorted colors if possible)
2 gallons apple cider or apple juice
Oatmeal cookies (see page 158 and double the recipe)

WINTER MENU:

Vegetarian Chili (see page 135 and triple the recipe)
24 taco shells
2 large bags corn chips
Small head lettuce, shredded
1 pound vegan cheese, shredded
2 large onions, finely chopped
Large bottle hot sauce
12 large baked potatoes
Hot Apple Cider (see page 104 and double the recipe)
Coconut Clusters (see page 157 and double the recipe)

SPRING MENU:

Tofu Eggless Salad (see page 140 and double the recipe)
Mock "Tuna" Salad (see page 118 and double the recipe)
Cucumber Salad (see page 108 and double the recipe)
2 large boxes vegan bread sticks
White Bean Spread (see page 155 and double the recipe)
2 large loaves whole wheat bread and 1-1/2 dozen rolls
6 tangerines
6 oranges
6 large bananas
2 pints strawberries
6 apples
2 gallons assorted fruit juices

Vegan Meal Plan

If you are in doubt about your diet, you can use this plan prepared by Ruth Ransom, R.D. and updated by Reed Mangels, Ph.D, R.D. as a GENERAL GUIDE. Consult a dietitian or medical doctor knowledgeable about nutrition for special needs.

A. PROTEIN FOODS: 5-6 SERVINGS PER DAY (7 FOR PREGNANT WOMEN; 8 FOR BREASTFEEDING WOMEN)

1. one serving equals:
> 1/2 cup cooked dried beans or peas
> 1/2 cup cooked soybeans*
> 1/2 cup tofu
> 1/2 cup tofu with calcium* (read label)
> 1/2 cup tempeh*
> 1 cup calcium-fortified soymilk** (counts as 2 starred food items)
> 1/4 cup almonds*, cashews, walnuts, pecans, or peanuts
> 2 Tablespoons peanut butter, tahini*, or almond butter*
> 1 ounce meat analog (veggie burger, veggie dog, deli slices, etc.)
> 1/4 cup soynuts*

B. WHOLE GRAINS: AT LEAST 6-8 SERVINGS/DAY

1. one serving equals:
> 1 slice whole wheat, rye, or whole grain bread
> 1 buckwheat or whole wheat pancakes or waffle
> 1 two-inch piece cornbread
> 2 Tablespoons wheat germ
> 1 ounce wheat or oat bran
> 1/4 cup sunflower*, sesame, or pumpkin seeds
> 3/4 cup wheat, bran, or corn flakes
> 1/2 cup oatmeal or farina
> 1/2 cup cooked brown rice, barley, bulgur, or corn
> 1/2 cup whole wheat noodles, macaroni, or spaghetti

C. VEGETABLES: AT LEAST 2-3 SERVINGS/DAY

1. at least 1 serving/day of the following:
    1 cup cooked or 2 cups raw broccoli*, bok choy*,Brussels sprouts, collards*, kale*, mustard greens*, chard, spinach, romaine lettuce, carrots, sweet potatoes, winter squash, or tomatoes

2. at least 1 serving/day (1 serving equals 1 cup cooked or 2 cups raw) of any other vegetable

D. FRUITS: 2-6 SERVINGS/DAY

1. two servings/day of the following:
    3/4 cup berries, 1/4 cantaloupe, 1 orange, 1/2 grapefruit, 1 lemon or lime, 1/2 papaya, 4-inch x 8-inch watermelon slice, or 1/2 cup orange, grapefruit, or calcium-fortified orange* juice, or vitamin C-enriched juice

2. additional servings as desired of other fruits:
    1 medium piece fresh fruit
    3/4 cup grapes
    1/2 cup cooked fruit or canned fruit without sugar
    1/4 cup raisins, dates, or dried fruit

E. FATS: 0-4 SERVINGS/DAY

1. one serving equals:
    1 teaspoon vegan margarine or oil
    2 teaspoons mayonnaise or salad dressing
    1 Tablespoon vegan cream cheese, gravy, or cream sauce

F. OMEGA-3 FATS: 2 SERVINGS/DAY

1. one serving equals:
    1 teaspoon flaxseed oil
    3 teaspoons canola or soybean oil
    1 Tablespoon of ground flaxseed
    1/4 cup walnuts

G. STARRED * FOOD ITEMS: 8 OR MORE SERVINGS/DAY; 10 OR MORE SERVINGS/DAY FOR THOSE AGE 51 & OLDER
(Also counts as servings from other groups.)

H. VITAMIN B12 SOURCES: 3 SERVINGS/DAY (4 FOR PREGNANT OR BREASTFEEDING WOMEN)

1. one serving equals:
> 1 Tablespoon Red Star Vegetarian Support Formula nutritional yeast
> 1 cup fortified soymilk
> 1 ounce fortified breakfast cereal
> 1-1/2 ounces fortified meat analogs

(Note: if these foods are not eaten regularly, a vitamin B12 supplement of 5-10 micrograms daily or 2,000 micrograms weekly should be used.)

I. ADDITIONAL COMMENTS

1. Additional servings from one or more food groups may be needed to meet energy needs especially for pregnant and breastfeeding women and physically active people.

2. This meal plan is for vegan adults. Meal plans for children can be found on our website: www.vrg.org

3. Items listed under Omega-3 Fats can also count as servings from the fats or protein foods groups, as appropriate.

	BREAKFAST	LUNCH	DINNER	SNACKS
SAMPLE TWO DAY MENU				
DAY 1	Peanut butter on toast Fortified orange juice	Bean burritos Carrot and celery sticks Strawberries	Stir-fry with tofu, broccoli, and bok choy Brown rice Ginger snaps	Popcorn sprinkled with nutritional yeast Fortified soymilk
DAY 2	Cold cereal with fortified soymilk Banana	Split pea soup Crackers with almond butter Coleslaw Fresh fruit	Pasta with lentil-spinach-tomato sauce French bread Steamed kale Cantaloupe	Trail mix with soy nuts and raisins Fortified orange juice

Vegetarianism on the Job

A common problem vegetarians encounter is finding something to eat while working. Cafeterias often offer very little food that we can consume besides salads or perhaps a veggie burger. As a result, vegetarians must often bring their own lunch. What happens when you have to attend a business luncheon or travel? The following essays are true stories written by those in the working world that have learned to cope in a meat-eating world. We also include ideas for adults whose job is to raise children.

COMPUTER PROGRAMMER

I work in a building with 300 employees, so our cafeteria has limited selections (almost all of which are not vegan). To save time, I bring my lunch to work every day rather than go out.

I don't like to spend a lot of time during the week preparing lunches, so I try to do any cooking on the weekend. I prepare double or triple batches of vegetarian chili, split pea soup, black bean soup, or lentil soup. Then I freeze individual portions. During the week, I grab one of the items from the freezer and add an apple, a microwaved potato, or half a sandwich. I'll also take leftover spaghetti.

Fortunately, I have a bread machine, which makes preparing delicious whole wheat vegan breads easy. I'll make a loaf on Sunday night and it lasts me throughout the week. Sometimes, I'll also use leftover bagels for lunch that I have put in the freezer.

When I don't take the time to cook in advance, I'll go for convenience foods such as Fantastic Foods soups where you simply add boiling water or frozen vegan entrées in various flavors such as Indian, Mexican, or Thai.

REGISTERED DIETITIAN

I've been a nutritionist for over 17 years, but I've been a vegetarian much longer. You would think that vegetarianism would be more prevalent among those who make diet and health their business, but that's not the case.

I'm non-traditional among those in my profession in another way, too. I have a home-based business and make my living as a nutrition consultant. Most of my time is spent in my home office, sitting at my desk, phoning, faxing, and word processing on my computer. My schedule is my own, and that means that I may eat breakfast, lunch, and dinner at times that may be totally out of sync with the outside world.

Others may not see what I eat when I'm working at home, but I keep myself in line. I spend very little time preparing lunch — under 10 minutes — because I'm busy and like to get back to work quickly. Sometimes I heat up leftovers from dinner the night before. Examples may be a slice or two of cheeseless vegetable pizza, a serving of a bean and vegetable casserole, or leftover Chinese take-out. I also like to reheat plain leftover vegetables (especially steamed kale or sweet potatoes) and I eat that with a couple of slices of whole wheat toast and a glass of orange juice. Sometimes I buy fresh carrot juice from the supermarket and mix that with orange juice. It's a delicious blend, and it always seems like a magically healthful "elixir" to me. I don't skimp when it comes to good quality food, and I keep a wide variety on hand.

On the other hand, I've also been known to have a bowl of cereal with soy milk for lunch, especially when I have a favorite kind in the cupboard. I'm a big fan of cereal (dry or hot). Sometimes I even eat it for dessert. Other days, I may cook a potato in the microwave and eat it with ketchup or salsa along with a toasted bagel or English muffin. Another favorite is a sweet potato cooked in the microwave, then topped with a little brown sugar and several "squeezes" of fresh lime juice.

I usually have hummus in my 'fridge, so some days I'll eat that in whole grain pita pockets. Another staple is a bag of baby carrots (the kind that are already peeled), and I'll eat a handful of those, dipped in hummus, along with a peanut butter and banana sandwich. Another common lunch is a big pasta bowl filled with mesclun salad mix. I add about a half cup of garbanzo beans, sliced tomatoes (if they're in season), a few black olives, and some ground black pepper. I top it with flavored vinegar (mango or raspberry vinegar are my favorites). I eat a slice of toast with that, or a piece of fresh fruit.

I care about the quality and presentation of my food. I eat a lot of plain, fresh foods prepared very simply. I take care to make my plate look attractive and even add a garnish now and then — even though it's only me who sees it! I may not spend much time preparing my meals, but I eat very well and enjoy my food immensely.

TEST SATISTICIAN

In the summer I bring cut up fresh tomatoes and make a lettuce and tomato sandwich on whole wheat bread that I bring from home. Otherwise, I eat at the salad bar at work.

During the winter months, I bring hummus, baba ghanouj, or soy cream cheese and tomato sandwiches on whole wheat bread. When I'm rushed I have to resort to the salad bar at work. I may also bring leftover baked potatoes that I microwave. This is typical. On occasion, when I have leftover pasta salads from home, I'll bring that, too.

MUSIC THEORIST AND ADMINISTRATOR

I bring a 1/2 cup of cottage cheese, 2 cups popcorn, and half an apple to work for lunch. I'll also bring a caffeine-free diet soda. (About once a week I go buy a cookie, too!)

WRITER/EDITOR

When I eat lunch, I'm usually at one of three locations: home, an office, or a sporting event. If I'm at home, I may eat small snacks all day (fruit, granola, peanut butter and crackers, etc.) and work right through lunch. If I do sit down to lunch at home, it's frequently comprised of the previous evening's leftovers. I keep whole wheat pitas and tortillas handy at all times and will usually fill a pita or roll a tortilla with leftover grains, vegetables, crumbled tofu or tempeh. Then I just heat and eat. Sometimes, I'll also spread hummus or refried beans on the pita or tortilla and once in a while I'll have a salad or bowl of hot soup on the side.

If I'm at one of the offices where I occasionally work, I might bring some leftovers, a sandwich or a packaged cup of soup or pasta. If not, I'll get a sandwich at a nearby deli or sub shop. A couple of slices of whole wheat bread loaded with vegetables and some hot peppers is a favorite. A few nearby restaurants serve veggie burgers, so I make that an occasional choice. Take-out orders from nearby Thai, Chinese, Italian, Indian, or Mexican eateries fit easily into my eating style. One of my favorite take-out items is a pizza covered with tomato sauce and basil, and dotted with chunks of falafel. Admittedly, you won't find this option at most pizza places, but if you love falafel, you should try creating this work of art at home.

Most of the sporting events I cover are at night, so I'm usually scrambling for dinner options on those evenings. From time to time I do find myself at a matinee hockey game. The home team provides a free meal to the working press two or three hours before game time. Usually this meal consists of the dead critter of the day accompanied by some form of potato, some overly steamed vegetables, a skimpy iceberg lettuce salad, and white rolls. Doesn't exactly make your taste buds dance, does it? If pressed for time, I might suffer through the wilted veggies, the salad, and the potatoes. But more often I'll pack a sandwich and some fruit to eat or try to eat a light lunch at a nearby restaurant. Another option is eating a large, late breakfast and bringing along fruit, granola, crackers, and other light snack items.

EDUCATIONAL TESTING SPECIALIST

I generally have a salad from the salad bar in our cafeteria or two to three hot side dishes such as rice with Brussels sprouts or kale, baked potatoes, or mushrooms. I also eat peanut butter and jelly sandwiches or cheese and onion or lettuce, tomato, and onion sandwiches. Sometimes I have a slice of pizza or a dish of pasta. I also like to bring celery and carrot sticks or an apple for snacks (when I remember to cut up the veggies).

EDUCATION RESEARCHER

I don't like to cook and I don't have a lot of time in the morning to put a bag lunch together. My lunch consists of putting my hand in my freezer and pulling out a Veggie Pocket — they come in several different varieties. I throw a handful of baby carrots in a plastic bag (which I reuse) and take a piece of fruit or two: apples and pears in the fall and winter; peaches and plums in the summer. At lunchtime, I just pop my Veggie Pocket in the microwave for 90 seconds and voila, lunch!

MATHEMATICIAN

I used to have hummus on pita brad and sometimes yogurt or salad. Ocassionally, I'll bring vegetarian cup-of-soups where you can add water and microwave them or add boiling water.

Lately I've been having peanut butter crackers along with a granola bar and juice. I don't typically eat a lot for lunch and I go through different phases.

ACCOUNTANT

My first job after graduating from college was for an accounting firm. At previous jobs, and throughout my life as a student, my vegetarian lifestyle was not a problem to deal with on a daily basis. I either brought my lunch with me or I ate at a place that I knew had vegetarian options available. While working for the accounting firm, however, I was often forced to be more flexible with my eating habits.

Most of the time, I worked at our clients' places of business. Therefore, I was not able to bring my lunch and I often had to go out to eat. Fortunately, I was often able to eat a decent meal. Other times, I needed to be a bit more creative with what I ordered for lunch. On several occasions, I worked at businesses located in small towns that had only one or two eating places. Most of these places were sandwich shops or family restaurants whose only vegetarian options were cheese subs or salads. It was during this time that I began to order what I call a PLT sandwich. This is made of peppers, lettuce, and tomato with the occasional addition of mushrooms when they are available. During one engagement, the only place where we could eat was at this little sandwich shop on the corner across the street. They had a selection of bagel sandwiches, all of which had meat or cheese on them. I ended up asking if they could make me a bagel sandwich with lettuce, tomatoes, and mushrooms. I was amazed at how ordering these sandwiches could cause such a crisis for the people who worked in the restaurant. In the end, however, no one ever denied me my "special orders" and many times I ended up getting a great bargain on the price. One woman who waited on me actually said she might like to try a PLT and that they would even consider adding it to their menu!

My co-workers were often curious about my lifestyle. Initially, a few of them would make sarcastic comments, attempting to make me get angry and defensive about my beliefs. After getting past the "Vegan, what is that?" stage, I believe most of my co-workers have grown to realize that stereotypes are nothing more than blatant generalizations. For just as not every accountant is a boring pocket-protector wearing business person, not every vegetarian looks down upon meat-eating people. As my co-workers learned more about my lifestyle choices, many of them grew to respect me for standing up for what I believe. At the same time, there will always be some people who have absolutely no interest in vegetarianism and I will always respect their freedom to choose their lifestyle. I have learned that the best way for vegetarians to educate others about vegetarianism is to simply live our lives according to our beliefs. There is no good reason to force our opinions on other people. If someone is curious about vegetarianism, they will approach us.

In general, the more often I ate in restaurants, the more I came to realize that there definitely are options available for both vegetarians and vegans. The key to discovering these options is to ask. Although the number of vegetarians is increasing, the majority of people are not vegetarian and menus are merely a reflection of this. However, most restaurants are quite willing to accommodate vegetarians. Regardless of our dietary preferences, we are still paying customers. With creativity and flexibility, eating out while on the job is actually quite simple. I have never expected to be able to order tempeh stroganoff or tofu cheesecake, but I have not had a problem ordering a salad with a baked potato, a few fruit cups to make a fruit salad, or a few side dishes of vegetables for a lunch platter. The best way vegetarians can encourage a restaurant to offer vegetarian dishes on their menu is to continue to request them. Only then can we expect to see more changes.

PARENTS

Lunchtimes are often not sit-down affairs, at least not for me. With two young children stating, "Could I please have more soymilk," "I want (whatever mom is eating," and of course, "I'm through and I need my hands washed (right as mom sits down to eat)" are some of the usual sounds.

So, my criteria for lunch foods are those that are quick to prepare. When my children were younger, I ate a lot of peanut butter. It was quick, it was filling, and it was often what I was fixing for them. We ate PB on bagels (cinnamon raisin bagels are best), PB sandwiches, PB on bananas, and PB on apples. Oh, yes, PB on crackers, too.

Leftovers, are another good, quick lunch. I usually try to have leftovers from dinner as one lunch option. They're often eaten straight out of the refrigerator or they can be reheated in a microwave. My personal favorites are soups, cold vegetables, and pasta.

I often make shakes for the children and may have some myself. These are made by combining half a package of silken soft tofu, some soy milk, a frozen banana or other fruit (strawberries, blueberries, peaches, applesauce, etc.), and maple syrup to taste in the food processor. Leftover frozen dessert (sorbet, Rice Dream, etc.) can also be added. These are good with bread or crackers on the side.

Hummus or some other kind of bean dip is also pretty quick. I eat this in pita bread, with crackers, on a bagel, or with vegetables and apples as dippers.

In the summer, my favorite lunch is a sliced tomato, still warm from the garden, on whole-grain bread or a bagel with spicy mustard. I could live on this!

If breakfast was a hurried affair, I may have a bowl of cold cereal with soy milk and fruit or some oatmeal for lunch. This is always amusing to the children.

My husband is also home during the day. His favorite quick lunches are leftovers, Tofu Pups, and Harvest Burgers. He always takes advantage of the garden in the summer and has veggie sandwiches and salads. And of course, there are the "immediate leftovers" from the children (crusts, rejected special of the day, and anything designated as "yucky."

Nutrient Charts

On the next few pages you will find charts listing good sources of some nutrients for vegans. You can find information about the nutrient content of common food items in the USDA Nutrient Database for Standard Reference. This can be found online at <http://www.nal.usda.gov/fnic/foodcomp>.

The Recommended Dietary Allowances (RDA) are the amounts of nutrients recommended by the Food and Nutrition Board, and are considered adequate for maintenance of good nutrition in healthy persons in the United States.

Please note that in an equal amount of calories, greens such as kale and collards have more calcium, iron, and protein than beef. The key to a healthy vegetarian diet is to eat a wide variety of foods. If you were eating only meat and no vegetables, you would have a hard time meeting your dietary needs.

Vegan Sources of Calcium

Food, serving size	Calcium (milligrams)
Almond butter, 2 TB	86
Bok choy , cooked, 1 cup	167-188
Broccoli, cooked , 1 cup	79
Calcium-fortified orange juice, 1/2 cup	150
Calcium-fortified soy milk, 1 cup	200-300
Collard greens, cooked, 1 cup	357
Figs, dried, 5	137
Kale, cooked, 1 cup	99
Tofu with calcium (read label), 1/2 cup	120-430
Adequate Intake (AI)	1000 (19-50 year olds)
	1200 (> 50 years old)

Vegan Sources of Iron

Food, serving size	Iron (milligrams)
Garbanzo beans, cooked, 1/2 cup	2.4
Kidney beans, cooked, 1/2 cup	2.6
Lentils, cooked, 1/2 cup	3.3
Oatmeal, instant, 1 packet	4.0
Pumpkin seeds, 2 TB	2.5
Soybeans, cooked, 1/2 cup	4.4
Spinach, cooked, 1/2 cup	3.2
Textured vegetable protein, reconstituted, 1/2 cup	2.7
Tofu, firm, 1/2 cup	6.6
Recommended Dietary Allowance (RDA)	14 (vegetarian men and postmenopausal women)
	33 (vegetarian premenopausal women)

Vegan Sources of Zinc

Food, serving size	Zinc (milligrams)
Fortified breakfast cereal, 1 oz	0.7-15
Garbanzo beans, cooked, 1/2 cup	1.3
Peas, cooked, 1/2 cup	1.0
Tahini, 2 TB	1.4
Tofu, firm, 1/2 cup	1.4
Veggie "meats", fortified, 1 oz	1.2-2.3
Wheat germ, 2 TB	2.3
Recommended Dietary Allowance (RDA)	11 (men)
	8 (women)

Note: Some vitamin D can be made by exposure to sunlight but varies according to season and latitude. (See next page for vitamin D food sources.)

Vegan Sources of Vitamin D

Food, serving size	Vitamin D (micrograms)
Fortified breakfast cereal, 1 oz	0.5-1.0
Fortified soy milk, 1 cup	1.0-3.0
Adequate Intake (AI)	5 (19-50 years old)
	10 (51-70 years old)
	15 (>70 years old)

Vegan Sources of Vitamin B-12

Food, serving size	Vitamin B-12 (micrograms)
Fortified breakfast cereal, 1 oz	0.6-6.0
Fortified soy milk, 1 cup	0.0-3.0
Vegetarian Support Formula Nutritional Yeast, 1 TB	4.0
Veggie "meats", fortified, 2.2 ounces	1.2
Recommended Dietary Allowance (RDA)	2.4 (adults)

Vegan Sources of Protein

Food, serving size	Protein (grams)
Bagel, 1	6
Brown rice, cooked, 1 cup	4.9
Garbanzo beans, cooked, 1 cup	14.5
Lentils, cooked, 1 cup	17.9
Peanuts, 1 oz	7.3
Soymilk, 1 cup	6.6
Tofu, 1/2 cup	10
Recommended Dietary Allowance (RDA)	56 (men)
	46 (women)

Spices For Vegetarian Cookery

Types and amounts of spices will vary according to your cooking style. Below are some combinations that have proved to work well. Experiment and enjoy!

ALLSPICE

cakes
breads
baked fruit
beverages

CELERY SEED

soups
coleslaw
potato salad
casseroles
mayonnaise

CHILI POWDER

stews
bean dishes

CINNAMON

oatmeal
breads
teas
apple dishes
cottage cheese
fruit dishes

CUMIN

Mexican dishes
spreads
chili

CURRY POWDER

Indian dishes
rice dishes
tofu
salads

GARLIC POWDER

Italian dishes
beans
salads
vegetables
soups
dips and spreads

MARJORAM

stews
squash
soups

MINT

vegetables
frozen desserts
tea
tabbouli

NUTMEG

apple pie
cheese dishes
desserts

OREGANO

beans
pizza
Mexican dishes
tomato dishes
vegetables
Italian dishes
chili

PAPRIKA

hash browns
vegetables
salads
rice
casseroles
cottage cheese

PARSLEY

salads
bread stuffing
dips
soups
stews

ROSEMARY

dips and spreads
vegetables
soups

TARRAGON

green salads
tomato dishes

THYME

peas and carrots
cheese dishes
onion soup

Egg Replacers (Binders)

Any of the following can be used to replace eggs:
- 1 small banana for 1 egg (great for cakes, pancakes, etc.)
- 2 Tablespoons cornstarch or arrowroot starch for 1 egg
- Ener-G Egg Replacer (or similar product available in health food stores or by mail order)
- 1/4 Cup tofu for 1 egg (blend tofu smooth with the liquid ingredients before they are added to the dry ingredients.)
- 1 Tablespoon ground flaxseed mixed with 3 Tablespoons water for 1 egg

Dairy Substitutes

The following can be used as dairy substitutes in cooking:
- soy milk (add 1 Tablespoon lemon juice or white vinegar to 1 cup soy milk to replace buttermilk in a recipe)
- soy margarine
- soy yogurt (found in health food stores)
- nut milks (blend nuts with water and strain)
- rice milks (blend cooked rice with water)

Meat Substitutes

- tempeh (cultured soybeans with a chewy texture)
- tofu (freezing and then thawing gives tofu a meaty texture; the tofu will turn slightly off white in color)
- wheat gluten or seitan (made from wheat and has the texture of meat; available in health food or Asian stores)
- dried beans
- textured soy protein (1/2 cup dry textured soy protein rehydrated in 1/2 cup boiling water can substitute for 1 cup ground beef)
- Veggie ground round

True or False?

1. Vegetarians have to worry about combining proteins.

2. Milk is the only good source of calcium.

3. Vegans should be aware of good sources of vitamin B12.

4. To be a vegetarian, I have to shop in a health food store and spend a lot of money on groceries.

5. Vegetarian cooking is complicated. I have to change my whole lifestyle to be a vegetarian.

6. Becoming a vegetarian will help me lose weight.

7. Animals in most food advertisements are smiling because they enjoy the good treatment given on farms.

ANSWERS:

1. **FALSE** Vegetarians easily meet their protein needs by eating a varied diet, as long as they consume enough calories to maintain their weight. It is not necessary to plan combinations of foods. A mixture of proteins throughout the day will provide enough essential amino acids. (See "Position of The American Dietetic Association and Dietitians of Canada: Vegetarian Diets," Journal of the American Dietetic Association, June 2003.)

In using the concept of limiting amino acids, many people wrongly assumed this meant there was none of that amino acid in the food. In fact, most foods contain some of all essential amino acids. Exceptions are some fruits and empty calorie or junk foods.

Another important fact is that the body maintains a relatively constant supply of essential amino acids in what is called the amino acid pool. This pool is made up of amino acids from endogenous sources (digestive secretions and desquamated cells) with only a small portion from the diet. The ability of the body to recycle amino acids reassures us that essential amino acids do not need to be eaten in any specific pattern of mealtime or type of food.

Again, the points to remember are to consume a variety of wholesome foods including some protein-rich vegetables and obtain sufficient calories.

2. **FALSE** One cup of whole milk has about 276 milligrams of calcium. One cup of cooked collard greens has 357 milligrams of calcium. Other foods including bok choy, kale, and fortified soymilk and juice also supply calcium.

3. **TRUE** If you do not consume eggs or dairy products, B-12 can easily be obtained from fortified foods such as Red Star's Vegetarian Support Formula brand of nutritional yeast and some fortified breakfast cereals, soymilks, and fake meats. As in any diet, it is helpful to read labels.

4. **FALSE** You can continue to shop at your local supermarket. If you stay away from processed foods and out-of-season fruits and vegetables, a vegetarian diet will probably be much cheaper than a meat-based diet. Compare the price of a salad bar to a steak dinner!

5. **FALSE** Like every other diet, vegetarianism can be complicated or simple. You can continue to eat out and order foods such as eggplant subs, spaghetti, salad bars, baked potatoes, and so on. An added bonus is that you probably will save money by ordering these types of dishes.

6. **FALSE** Again, a vegetarian diet is like any other diet. If you have a normal metabolism, and over consume high-calorie foods such as peanut butter, avocados, nuts, and rich desserts, and do not burn up these excess calories, you will probably gain weight no matter what the sources of these calories.

7. **FALSE** In our observations of animals before slaughter, we have not seen any smiling animals. In order to raise animals for food economically, the animals are kept in crowded conditions. Cows are penned up for several months before slaughter without being allowed to exercise. This prevents the meat from becoming tough. One chicken house could easily contain thousands of chickens, who have very short lives, and do not get to see outside sunlight. Factory farm animals are usually fed antibiotics to prevent illnesses.

Join The Vegetarian Resource Group and Receive Vegetarian Journal

Name _____

Address _____

_____ Zip Code _____

__ Enclosed is $20 for VRG membership and 1-year subscription to Vegetarian Journal.

__ Please charge my (circle one) MasterCard/Visa
     # _____ Expires:____/____

Send payment and subscription information to The Vegetarian Resource Group, PO Box 1463, Baltimore, MD 21203. Or fax this form to (410) 366-8804. You can charge your membership over the phone by calling (410) 366-8343 Mon.-Fri. 9am to 5pm EST. Additionally, you can join VRG or purchase books on our website at <**www.vrg.org**>. E-mail vrg@vrg.org with any questions.

Simply Vegan – Quick Vegetarian Meals

The immensely popular Simply Vegan, by Debra Wasserman and Reed Mangels, PhD, RD, features over 160 vegan recipes that can be prepared quickly, as well as an extensive nutrition section. The chapters cover topics on protein, fat, calcium, iron, vitamin B12, pregnancy and the vegan diet, and raising vegan kids. Additionally, the book (224 pages) includes sample menus and meal plans. To order, send $18 (including postage) to The Vegetarian Resource Group, PO Box 1463, Baltimore, MD 21203.

To Order More Copies of Meatless Meals for Working People

Send $15 (including postage) for each book to VRG, PO Box 1463, Baltimore, MD 21203 or call (410) 366-8343; 9am to 5pm Mon.-Fri. EST.

Visit our Website <www.vrg.org>

Index

Mayonnaise, Eggless
Coleslaw, 107
Mock "Tuna" Salad,
118
Potato Salad and
Olives, 110
Tofu Eggless Salad,
140
Tofu Spinach Dip, 140

McDonald's, 48

Meat Substitutes, 180

**Menu, Sample Two
Day**, 166

**Menus for Females,
51+ Years Old**, 84

**Menus for Females,
19-50 Years Old**, 69

**Menus for Males,
51+ Years Old**, 91

**Menus for Males,
19-50 Years Old**, 76

Mexican Fiesta, 149

Mexican Succotash,
149

Milk Shake, 106

Mint, 179

Mock Foo Young, 147

Mock "Tuna" Salad,
118

Moe's Southwest Grill,
50

**Mono- and Digly-
cerides**, 36

**Mushroom/Eggplant
Spread**, 153

Mushrooms
Chopped "Liver"
Spread, 154
Cream of Broccoli
Soup, 116

Fried Rice with Pea-
nuts or Almonds, 148
Mushroom/Eggplant
Spread, 153
Sautéed Mushrooms,
125
Spaghetti and Vege-
table Sauce, 136
Spinach/Mushroom
Sandwich, 118
Stuffed Mushrooms,
127

Mustard
Tofu Spinach Dip, 140

Natural Flavors, 36

Noodles & Company,
51

Nut "Cheese," 156

Nutmeg, 179

Nutrient Charts, 175

Nutritional Yeast
Pasta Dish, 129

**Oatmeal/Apples/Rai-
sins and Cinnamon**,
100

Oatmeal Cookies, 158

Oats
Creamed Zucchini/
Potato Soup, 117
Eggless Banana Pan-
cakes, 102
Oatmeal/Apples/Rai-
sins and Cinnamon,
100
Oatmeal Cookies, 158

Olives
Potato Salad and
Olives, 110
Raw Vegetable Platter,
162

Omega-3 Fats, 165

Onions
Creamed Carrot Soup,
116

Curried Tofu with Pea-
nuts, 144
Easy Tostadas, 150
Fresh Tomato Soup,
115
Fried Rice with Pea-
nuts or Almonds, 148
Leftover Potato Dish,
124
Lentil Pate, 152
Lentil Stew, 138
Ratatouille, 136
Refried Beans, 149
Rigatoni Combination,
130
Sautéed Mushrooms,
125
Spaghetti and Vege-
table Sauce, 136
Spinach Pie, 142
Sweet and Sour
Cabbage, 128
Tofu Spinach Dip, 140
Vegetable Pot Pie, 134
Vegetarian Chili, 135

Orange Juice
Blended Fruit Drink,
104
Red Beet Dressing,
114

Oranges
Applesauce, 99
Sweet French Dress-
ing, 113

Oregano, 179

Papa John's, 52

Paprika, 179

Parsley
Creamed Carrot Soup,
116
Creamed Zucchini/
Potato Soup, 117
Pasta Dish, 129
Potato Pancakes, 120
Summer Tofu Salad,
141
Tofu Burgers, 142
Vegetable Rice Soup,
115
Vegetarian Stew, 132

Parsley, 179

Great Resources from The VRG!

Online Version of Vegetarian Journal's Guide to Natural Foods Restaurants

Going on a trip? Get the most up-to-date listings for vegetarian, vegan, or veggie-friendly restaurants from the online version of Vegetarian Journal's Guide to Natural Foods Restaurants in the U.S. and Canada. Just visit <www.vrg.org/restaurant/index.htm> to find details about establishments in all 50 U.S. states, all of Canada's provinces and territories, and Puerto Rico!

The VRG Parents' List

Are you raising a vegetarian or vegan child? If so, join The VRG Parents' List on Yahoo! Groups and begin exchanging ideas with more than 1,000 other moms and dads of veggie kids. Discussions range from creating tasty snacks for toddlers to attending non-vegetarian gatherings, from helping kids handle peer pressure to shopping for leather and wool alternatives! You don't even need a Yahoo! ID to join, just an e-mail address. Go to <http://groups.yahoo.com/group/vrgparents/> to sign up!

VRG-NEWS E-Mail Newsletter

VRG-NEWS is a free electronic newsletter that provides subscribers with vegan recipes, fast food chain and ingredient updates, product reviews, announcements about new books and free samples, and all the latest news from VRG. This update keeps tens of thousands of readers current about veggie happenings until the next issue of Vegetarian Journal comes their way. See <www.vrg.org/vrgnews/index.htm> to subscribe!

To Join VRG or For More Information
Call (410) 366-8343 or Visit WWW.VRG.ORG!